Lindal Planning

BRINGING YOUR DREAM TO LIFE

Lindal
CEDAR HOMES

HARLACHER RESIDENCE, HI. CUSTOM HOME.

CONTENTS

Many photographs and floorplans are cross-referenced in Lindal Living ❶ or Lindal Planning ❷.

01

Bringing your dreams into focus

and putting them down on paper is one

5

of the pleasures of planning your Lindal Cedar Home. In this book, we'll help you take stock of your needs and desires. Share helpful tips on every aspect of home planning. And present over 80 of our latest plans — designs for living that are as smart as they are beautiful. Through more than 55 years and tens of thousands of projects, we've helped people transform their visions of home into personal expressions of lasting quality, style and craftsmanship. We're proud to share our design and engineering strengths, our attention to personal service, and our unwavering standards for the finest building materials. It's all here — and, like this book, it's dedicated to you.

Lindal Design & Engineering

Lindal design and Lindal engineering give your new home the best beginning — a lifetime of strength and beauty in every square foot. Whatever elements of style you choose, you can count on the structural integrity and design flexibility that have distinguished Lindal homes for more than half a century. And as you bring your dream to life, there's simply no better feeling than knowing your home is backed by the best guarantee in the industry.

DESIGNED FOR LIFE

Lindal's collection of exclusive homes gives you the best of both worlds: the proven success of designs that are the ultimate in livability and style — and the flexibility to personalize your favorite into the home of your dreams. Add a window or a wing. Expand a room. Change the roofline. Add a sunroom. Lindal's design consultation is one of the many services that distinguish our company — and your new home. Your local Lindal dealer is an expert in helping you progress from dream to design.

'BETTER THAN CODE'

Lindal's building system features dozens of top-of-the-line engineered details that often exceed local building practices and add exceptional strength and structural integrity. Each one makes a living difference in the lasting comfort, value and low maintenance of your home. Our floor system is just one example: Lindal uses first-rate engineering, technology and materials to design a floor system that stands up to a lifetime of everyday wear and tear — without getting loose or squeaky along the way.

OFTEN IMITATED; NEVER EQUALED

The fundamental strengths of a Lindal home cannot be copied — because they are exclusively Lindal. Company founder and industry leader Sir Walter Lindal holds an impressive array of U.S., Canadian and international patents for innovations that distinguish the building system and structural integrity of every Lindal home. And each Lindal plan is protected by copyright. As a homeowner, it's good to know that no one can build a Lindal design without the purchase of our high-quality materials,

which maintains Lindal as a highly respected and valued name in the home marketplace.

PLANNING FOR SUCCESS

One of the thrills of building your dream is watching it take shape on paper. Lindal's design sketches and preliminary plans make it easy to visualize your home and make modifications early on. Once you've approved your preliminary plans, your local Lindal dealer will send them to our corporate Design Department, where a team using computer aided design (CAD) technology

produces final construction documents that are clear, exact and easy for builders to use. Should your local building department require design modifications or structural engineering due to snow loads, wind loads or the number of windows in your home, Lindal's Engineering Department is at your service.

STATE-OF-THE-ART TECHNICAL SUPPORT

Lindal's advanced CAD technology lets us virtually build every home on our computer systems before a single board is cut to your specifications or delivered to your building site. It's a process that eliminates the surprises so

common in custom home building experiences — bringing precision, foresight and integrity to the final design of your home.

THE GUARANTEE OF A LIFETIME

The strengths of Lindal engineering and Lindal design support another rarity in today's home

building industry: a lifetime warranty against structural defects. It's by far the best guarantee in the industry. Lindal's Lifetime Structural Warranty gives you the assurance that one of life's most important investments is backed by a promise — and a company — you can count on.

OPPOSITE: LEFT Lindal builds confidence. Your Lindal home is covered by a Lifetime Structural Warranty, the best guarantee in the industry. RIGHT The innovations that distinguish Lindal's building systems and structural integrity were developed by company founder Sir Walter Lindal, who holds an impressive array of patents on the strengths that set Lindal homes apart. THIS PAGE: Using advanced CAD technology, any design issues and modifications can be easily visualized and resolved early on, eliminating change orders and other surprises that are common and costly in custom home construction.

Dealer Service

The quality of your new home will be directly related to the quality of the people involved — which is why so many people choose Lindal and their local independent Lindal dealer. Your Lindal team combines the hands-on expertise and attention of your local dealer with the experience, financial strength and quality assurance of a company that stands behind you from start to finish, and long afterward, too. It's a combination of professional excellence and personal attention you won't find anywhere else.

BUILD ON OUR KNOWLEDGE

Our dealers understand what builders need in order to meet budgets, deadlines and expectations. Whether you follow your builder's progress from a distance or hammer every nail yourself, you and your builder will appreciate all the things we do to make the entire process go as smoothly as possible.

PROMISES KEPT

From pinning down every planning detail to delivering a part-coded building package that's complete and on time, we've spent more than 55 years taking many of the uncertainties out of building a custom home. Your Lindal dealer can help you to focus your priorities and stay on track so that your scheduled move-in date can become a reality. In the building industry, Lindal reliability is one of the rarest commodities of all.

YOUR LOCAL ADVOCATE AND LINDAL EXPERT

Your local independent Lindal dealer can visit your site. Provide the assistance you need to turn your ideas into a working design. Analyze your plans for site suitability, functionality and aesthetics. Share the benefits of local building resources and code requirements. Oversee your order from the first plans through final delivery, and show you how to get the most home for your money — by putting it into the things that matter to you. Along the way, your dealer's expertise, attention and advocacy eliminate a lot of the problems that are common in creating a custom home. The service and support of your local Lindal dealer make a difference throughout every step of the planning process, and in the long-term satisfaction with your home.

SEE THE LIVING DIFFERENCE

A visit to your local Lindal Model Home or Lindal Design Center is the best way to experience the Lindal difference firsthand — the secrets of our success and, most importantly, your satisfaction.

ABOVE Your local independent Lindal dealer adds a depth of planning expertise, technical insight, local construction knowledge and project follow-through that is rare in today's home building industry.

Quality Materials

The beauty of building a Lindal is knowing it will be crafted of the finest building materials in the world, far superior to the quality typically available to builders at the local lumberyard. At a time when standards are declining and shortcuts are typical in the home building industry, Lindal quality is alive and well. We've found it never goes out of style — or demand. Because our name is synonymous with quality, Lindal homes often command high resale values in the marketplace. Take a look at how dramatically Lindal building materials differ from those used in the bulk of today's custom homes.

LINDAL CEDAR: A CLASS BY ITSELF

Here's the stuff dreams are made of: Lindal's fragrant, fine-grained Western red cedar. Kiln-dried, cut and planed to a radiant finish, Lindal cedar is one of nature's most perfect building materials: strong, resistant to moisture and insects — and a sensory delight. It gives your home a lifetime of low maintenance and lasting value.

CEDAR'S INNER STRENGTH

Under a microscope, a cross-section of cedar reveals the secret of its exceptional insulating ability: nearly ten million air-filled cells in every cubic inch. Cedar's uniform cell structure gives it twelve times the insulating value of stone or concrete. This uniformity at a cellular level also makes cedar easy to work with and stable against shrinking or swelling.

CONTROL FROM FOREST TO BUILDING SITE

Most lumber on the market isn't what it used to be — and much that passes industry grading doesn't make the grade at Lindal. The natural wonder of Lindal's finely crafted cedar comes through in everything from superior framing lumber to premium lengths of siding. Our above-grade quality control system means we reject much of the lumber that often ends up in even high-end custom homes.

KILN-DRYING MAKES A DIFFERENCE

Virtually all Lindal cedar is kiln-dried, which reduces and controls the moisture content. By taking the time to kiln-dry our cedar, we reduce the chance for twisting, warping and shrinking so common with green wood and air-dried lumber.

SUPERIOR STRUCTURAL MATERIALS

Much of the framing lumber and beam material that passes industry grading simply doesn't make the grade at Lindal. We set above-grade standards for our framing lumber, and enforce them with a stringent visual regrading system that greatly reduces the amount of waning, cupping and splitting. We specify premium architectural-grade, glue-laminated beams of the finest wood available. Our visual inspection keeps Lindal beams at the highest end of this premium grade. And every beam comes individually inspected and handwrapped — made-to-order for your home.

OTHERS' OPTIONS ARE LINDAL STANDARDS

As you get acquainted with Lindal quality, you'll find the details that cost extra with most new homes are standard with ours. For

example: Critical building components are part-numbered for easy reference to your blueprints and materials list. And Lindal's floor system, cedar siding and cedar lining come with tongue-and-groove fittings for easy installation.

TOP At our own facility, Lindal kiln-dries virtually every piece of cedar we use in our homes. Kiln-drying dramatically reduces the twisting, warping and shrinking found in green and air-dried lumber. BOTTOM Rigorous inspections for quality control on our end ensure satisfaction on yours.

02

It starts with a desire to build a home as great as all outdoors. A yearning to live every day, not just vacations, with your favorite view. A vision to transform a piece of property into a very private, very personal retreat that reflects what matters most to you. Every Lindal begins with a dream — the inspiration to imprint your style on your home, to shape your surroundings to your own sense of beauty and functionality, to experience the soul-satisfying rewards of a house that feels like home. Allowing yourself to realize this dream is what planning, and living, in a Lindal is all about.

11

Your Plan, Your Process

"WE CHOSE LINDAL BECAUSE IT PERMITTED US TO BE CREATIVE IN DEVELOPING A HOME THAT HAD FEATURES IMPORTANT TO US WITHOUT AN ARCHITECT'S ASSISTANCE."

— Harold & Brigid Wiking, McCall, Idaho

Many home planning experiences are an all-or-nothing affair when the fact is, most people are looking for a level of involvement that is somewhere in between. You'll find the perfect balance of flexibility and support at Lindal, where you can have as much or as little involvement as you wish in the planning process. At any point, your Lindal dealer is ready, willing and uniquely able to help you transform your personal wants and needs into floorplans and elevations.

CHOOSE A PROVEN SUCCESS

Many of our homeowners wouldn't change a thing about their favorite Lindal plan. If you prefer the savings, convenience, time-proven success and quick delivery of an existing plan, you've come to the right place. Lindal offers one of the world's widest selections of exclusive home styles and floorplans. You'll find many of our most popular plans in this book; your local Lindal dealer can show you an even wider selection.

PERSONALIZE YOUR FAVORITE PLAN

Whether you'd like to increase the size of your kitchen or change the exterior from clapboard to stucco, your local dealer will work closely with you to modify your favorite existing Lindal plan according to your wants and needs. Because much of the basic design has already been completed, modifying your favorite plan typically takes less time to design and ship than does a completely custom home.

OR BRING YOUR OWN DESIGN TO LIFE

Have a one-of-a-kind custom home in mind? Lindal can design your dream home or work with the architect of your choice; we're delighted to be part of your team. Either way, you can count on a level of engineering, building materials and craftsmanship you won't find anywhere else. A modest design fee, based on the square footage of your home, is all it takes to transform your unique ideas into working plans and final blueprints.

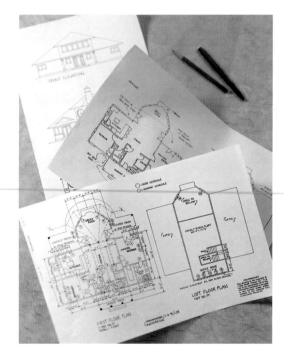

THIS PAGE: LEFT If you choose to work with an architect, we're happy to be part of your team. UPPER RIGHT When you're ready to begin moving from dream to design, turn to our collection of Lindal's most popular home plans, which begin on page 58 of this book. OPPOSITE Time and again, Lindal homeowners tell us their local Lindal dealer was a valuable source of inspiration, expertise and support that they wouldn't have had any other way.

Your Lifestyle Inventory

The process of planning your new home should be just as personal as the results — an expression of who you are and how you celebrate life. With that in mind, we invite you to complete Lindal's Lifestyle Inventory, a list of questions and considerations that will help you define your wants and needs. Armed with this self-knowledge, you'll find it a pleasure to begin the planning process, translating your ideas into a custom home that's a daily joy to live in. A friendly word of advice as you "take inventory": Don't edit your dreams too early or discard them as too ambitious. With the help of your local Lindal dealer, you'll be surprised how many of them will come to life.

1. Where and when do you gather with others in your home?
    _____
    _____

2. Do you read? If so, where and when? _____
    _____
    _____

3. Do you need a room for seclusion? _____

4. Do you collect anything? If so, what do you prefer to collect?
    _____
    _____

5. How do you spend time at home? Any hobbies? _____
    _____
    _____

6. Do you watch TV? If so, what are your television viewing routines?
    _____
    _____

7. In which room does your family watch television? _____

8. How many people usually gather to watch television together?
    _____

9. Do you like an open floorplan or traditionally divided floorplan?
    _____

10. How many children will be living at the residence? _____
    _____

11. Will you have frequent overnight guests? Grown children? College students? Grandparents? Grandchildren? _____
    _____

12. How often do you entertain? What's the size of a typical gathering? _____
    _____

13. Do you cook often? Does more than one person usually cook at a time? _____
    _____

14. Does your family like to eat any meals in the kitchen or do you prefer to eat in a more formal dining room? _____
    _____

15. Would you like your dream master bedroom located on the first floor or a second floor? _____

16. Describe your master bath. Do you want it to be compact and efficient or large and luxurious? Natural light? Separate shower?
    _____

17. Do you often take leisurely baths, whirlpools? _____

18. Do you want walk-in closets off your master bedroom? _____
    _____

19. Do you desire a home office, media room, study, music room? If so, describe the room(s) you envision. _____

_____

20. What preferences do you have for the style of your home? Classic Lindal soaring roof lines? Traditional styles such as Farmhouse, or Craftsman? Contemporary? _____

_____

21. Do you prefer one or two story homes? _____

22. Do you want a garage? Attached or detached? _____

_____

23. Which exterior siding do you prefer? Lindal Cedar horizontal or vertical, cedar shingles, clapboard, brick, stone, stucco, or a combination? _____

24. Are there any views you wish to capture? _____

_____

25. Do you want morning light in any particular room? _____

_____

26. Do you want sunset views from any particular room? _____

_____

27. Would you like access from a particular room to an outdoor area? _____

28. Do you want a deck, balcony or patio? Will you often eat outside?

_____

29. Do you have any health problems that would affect design or materials in your home? _____

_____

30. Does anyone in your family use a wheelchair? _____

_____

31. Would it be easier for some household members to use levers rather than doorknobs? _____

_____

Dreaming of a large, spa-like bath? A small, intimate dining room? The table below is a rule-of-thumb guide to selecting the size of the rooms in your home. Once you've chosen the approximate size you'd like each room to be, just tally them up to arrive at your home's total square footage.

ROOM	(A) SMALL	(B) MEDIUM	(C) LARGE
ENTRY	5' x 6' 30 SQ. FT.	8' x 10' 80 SQ. FT.	10' x 16' 160 SQ. FT.
KITCHEN	8' x 11' 88 SQ. FT.	10' x 13' 130 SQ. FT.	12' x 16' 192 SQ. FT.
NOOK	8' x 8' 64 SQ. FT.	10' x 10' 100 SQ. FT.	12' x 12' 144 SQ. FT.
DINING	10' x 12' 120 SQ. FT.	12' x 14' 168 SQ. FT.	12' x 16' 192 SQ. FT.
GREAT ROOM/ FAMILY ROOM	12' x 16' 192 SQ. FT.	14' x 18' 252 SQ. FT.	18' x 26' 468 SQ. FT.
FORMAL LIVING	11' x 14' 154 SQ. FT.	12' x 16' 192 SQ. FT.	14' x 18' 252 SQ. FT.
MASTER BEDROOM	12' x 12' 144 SQ. FT.	14' x 18' 252 SQ. FT.	16' x 20' 320 SQ. FT.
SECONDARY BEDROOM(S)	10' x 11' 110 SQ. FT.	12' x 14' 168 SQ. FT.	14' x 18' 252 SQ. FT.
BATH(S)	5' x 8' 40 SQ. FT.	6' x 10' 60 SQ. FT.	9' x 12' 108 SQ. FT.
LAUNDRY/ UTILITY ROOM	6' x 6' 36 SQ. FT.	6' x 10' 60 SQ. FT.	10' x 12' 120 SQ. FT.
GARAGE (2 CAR)	21' x 21' 441 SQ. FT.	23' x 23' 529 SQ. FT.	26' x 26' 676 SQ. FT.
GARAGE (3 CAR)	30' x 21' 630 SQ. FT.	34' x 24' 816 SQ. FT.	36' x 26' 936 SQ. FT.
SUBTOTAL A, B, C:			
TOTAL SQUARE FEET (A+B+C)=			

15

Siting Your Home

"I WANTED A HOUSE THAT WOULD FIT WITH THE ENVIRONMENT, BE OPEN AND TAKE ADVANTAGE
OF THE VIEWS AROUND US. THIS IS THE ULTIMATE HOUSE FOR ME."

— Betty Lindsey, Olsburg, Kansas

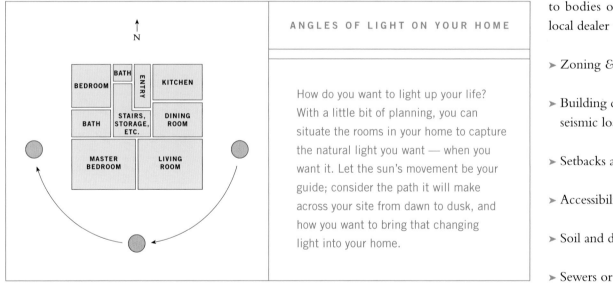

ANGLES OF LIGHT ON YOUR HOME

How do you want to light up your life? With a little bit of planning, you can situate the rooms in your home to capture the natural light you want — when you want it. Let the sun's movement be your guide; consider the path it will make across your site from dawn to dusk, and how you want to bring that changing light into your home.

The most beautiful and functional homes are a synergy of structure and site. Set aside time to identify the views you want to capture. Take a walk on your property at different times of day — and night. Note the ebb and flow of light, the sun's changing path, the way wind and air move across the site. Consider how changing seasons will affect it. Whether you're building on a steep hillside or a level lot, your Lindal dealer can help you arrive at a design and site orientation that create a sense of place and make the most of your property's topography, light, micro-climate and view potential.

DEVELOP A SITE PLAN

Once you're well acquainted with your site, your Lindal dealer can draw a working site plan. Sketch in property lines, ground slope, roads, power, water and gas mains, nearby buildings and any natural features — from trees to bodies of water. During this process, your local dealer will want to investigate:

➤ Zoning & covenants

➤ Building codes for snow, wind and seismic loads, and shoreline standards

➤ Setbacks and height restrictions

➤ Accessibility for trucks and equipment

➤ Soil and drainage tests

➤ Sewers or septic systems

➤ Proximity of electricity, gas, water, phone and cable TV

These factors may influence your home's design and site locations. In addition, they will definitely have an impact on cost. Your local Lindal dealer is an invaluable source of information. They can help you find the most cost effective solutions. The result: a home that feels like it belongs.

N

10' Sanitary Sewer Easement

102'   104'   106'   108'

Driveway

Street

30'

Lawn

PROPOSED
DWELLING

DECK

FUTURE
POOL

Telephone
Box

Water
Meters

Garage Drive

98'

100'

PROPERTY LINE — · — · — · —

TOPOGRAPHY LINE — ·· — ·· — ··

SET BACK LINE — — — — —

ENHANCE THE LAY OF YOUR LAND

FLAT LOT   STEEP LOT   SLOPED LOT

ENHANCE THE LAY OF YOUR LAND Lindal design and engineering lets you make the most of any site — and every view. It's all a matter of choosing a home design and site orientation that enhance your property's topography, light and view potential. Keep in mind that it makes more sense to adapt your design to the land than vice versa; excavating and grading are expensive pursuits that can undermine the character of the site you fell in love with. FLAT LOT This home shows its private side to the street, with easy, level access to the main entrance. STEEP LOT If your lot is on a steep slope, consider Lindal pole construction. SLOPED LOT The beauty of a daylight basement on a sloping view lot: a spectacular outlook from both levels.

A Floorplan that Flows

"OUR HOUSE WAS BUILT FOR ENTERTAINING. WE'VE CREATED A FLOW FROM OUR KITCHEN AND DINING ROOM
TO A STEP-DOWN SUNROOM. ALL ROOMS HAVE DOUBLE DOORS TO THE PATIO."

— *Bob & Judy Newsome, Woodstock, Vermont*

Some homes just seem to work beautifully —
and when they do, you can be sure a well
considered floorplan is underfoot. Your floorplan should make it easy and comfortable to go
through the motions of daily living. It should
also create natural and complementary relationships between rooms. Here's how to map out a
master plan that honors traffic patterns and
activity zones — creating a floorplan that makes
sense and feels right.

PLOT TRAFFIC PATTERNS

➤ Your main entry should allow you to enter
any room in the house without passing through
other rooms. Ideally, it gives guests easy access
to the rooms you use most for entertaining.

➤ The second entry should lead directly to the
kitchen. If you can include a place between this
entry and the kitchen to store coats and para-
phernalia, you'll be glad you did.

➤ Think about how each family member
spends the day and mentally walk through the
plan you're considering. Any hitches? Give
special attention to the type of daily chores that
a good floorplan can make easier and more
efficient — such as answering the door and
carrying in groceries.

CREATE ACTIVITY ZONES

➤ The best floorplans show respect for a household's basic activities — working, eating,
sleeping and entertaining — by situating them
in harmony with one another.

➤ Ideally, the noisiest zones, such as entertainment areas, are grouped together and well away
from sleeping areas. In a neighborhood, you
might want to locate your quiet zones toward
the rear of your home, away from street noises
and passersby. Naturally, your site, views and
surroundings also influence your decisions.

➤ Wherever possible, each bedroom should be
buffered from other bedrooms for the sake of
privacy and quiet. Closets, staircases and book-
shelves are effective sound barriers.

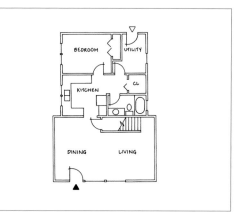

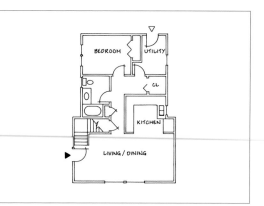

TOP Long before you have to live with the results, a few drawings can show you whether or not a floorplan works. This one clearly does not; the kitchen would be the site of regular "traffic jams." BOTTOM
This floorplan works; no need to cross through the kitchen in order to get somewhere else.

18

MASTER SUITE & BATH

There's a trend toward placing master suites on the main floor. Situate the door so the bath or closets can be reached without crossing the sleeping area. Consider integrating the bath, closets and dressing area into a suite of separate but connected spaces.

SECOND ENTRY

Life is easier when you have convenient access from the garage to your kitchen.

BEDROOMS

To give you the furniture arranging flexibility you need, bedrooms should have at least two walls uninterrupted by doors or low windows. Place closets or other buffers between rooms to reduce noise.

MAIN ENTRY

It should be inviting, and have easy access to the formal living area. The main entry should also be well-defined and centrally located. An entry closet is a daily convenience; so is easy access to other floors.

DINING ROOM

Proximity to the kitchen is key; many dining rooms have opened up to become part of a larger space that includes the kitchen and family room.

KITCHEN

You'll want your kitchen to be convenient to rooms where your family spends most of its time. If your cook likes to socialize with family and guests, consider opening the kitchen to other rooms.

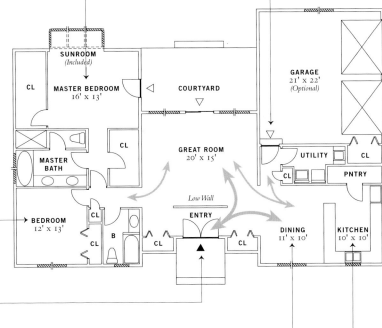

SUNROOM
(Included)

MASTER BEDROOM
16' x 13'

CL

COURTYARD

GARAGE
21' x 22'
(Optional)

CL

MASTER
BATH

CL

GREAT ROOM
20' x 15'

UTILITY

CL

CL

PNTRY

BEDROOM
12' x 13'

CL

Low Wall

ENTRY

CL

B

CL

CL

DINING
11' x 10'

KITCHEN
10' x 10'

Courtyard Living

BEDROOMS two

BATHROOMS 2 full

MASTER BEDROOM first floor

TOTAL AREA 1,739 sq. ft.

FIRST FLOOR 1,739 sq. ft.

SIZE 64' x 43'

View elevation

0 feet   10 feet   20 feet

1/16 inch represents 1 foot

Lindal

Your Custom Kitchen

The kitchen is the heart of most homes — a place to entertain friends, a focal point for family moments and memories, a nurturing spot where you can settle in for a great meal and good conversation. It's also the room that takes the most planning. Kitchens that work are a masterful mix of form and function with these underlying strengths: well thought-out traffic patterns, hard-working counters, islands and peninsulas; ample storage; low-maintenance materials; conveniently clustered work areas — and, increasingly, work centers for more than one cook.

➤ The classic rule of kitchen efficiency is worth remembering: Locate sink, cooktop and refrigerator in a triangle whose sides total less than 22 feet. But the shape of kitchens is changing; if there's often more than one cook in your kitchen, consider adding a workstation outside the triangle. Or break out of the triangle altogether with a shared work island and wide aisles that make it easy for two cooks to collaborate.

➤ Include plenty of counter and storage space on either side of the sink and stovetop. Make sure your access to the sink won't be blocked when the dishwasher door is open.

➤ Well-designed lighting makes a world of difference. Natural light dramatically increases a kitchen's aesthetic appeal and sense of connection to the rest of the house.

➤ Give yourself at least 10 feet of countertop space, excluding appliances. Space between counters should be 36 to 48 inches — 60 inches if there are often two cooks in your kitchen.

➤ Restaurant-grade ranges are increasingly popular in home kitchens, and easy to accommodate when you plan for them.

➤ Consider the virtues of a walk-in pantry, kitchen desk, handy "recycling center" and trash compactor — are they important to you?

➤ Plan for lots of storage, then double your estimate. You'll be glad you did.

➤ Consider a separate sink for salad preparation or a wet bar outside the work triangle.

➤ Position the refrigerator so the door opens away from the sink and cooktop.

➤ Lindal SkyWalls are a dramatic way to take in a view from your kitchen and add the ever-changing interest of natural light.

➤ Increasingly, kitchens are part of a larger, open space that allows an easy flow between food preparation, casual dining and relaxing.

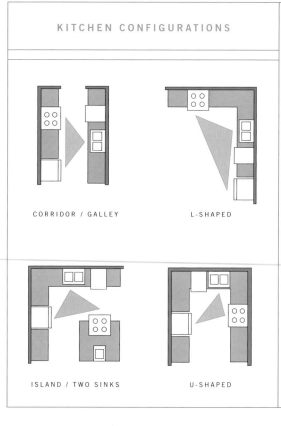

KITCHEN CONFIGURATIONS

CORRIDOR / GALLEY

L-SHAPED

ISLAND / TWO SINKS

U-SHAPED

CORRIDOR/GALLEY Two parallel counters adapt well to an open kitchen concept. The drawback: traffic can interrupt the work triangle.

L-SHAPED Two walls at right angles form an L, which supports an efficient triangle; traffic can pass by without interrupting the cook.

ISLAND/TWO SINKS Islands work well in large U and L layouts. They minimize the distance of the work triangle in big kitchens — and can double as eating bars.

U-SHAPED The ideal kitchen layout. The "dead end" eliminates traffic through the triangle, and two cooks can comfortably coexist.

PREVIOUS SPREAD A warm, inviting kitchen and adjacent dining area with cedar ceilings, lots of natural light and easy access to the deck. Hurlbutt residence, ID. Custom Pole. THIS PAGE: 1. Curved cherry cabinets create a formal feeling in this custom kitchen. Martin residence, NY. Custom home. 2. A work counter gets this kitchen's window view. Custom residence, NY. Chapel Hill plan. ◑ 93. 3. Lindal cedar lines a pitched ceiling; granite countertops and a tile floor add to the rich textural mix. Saunders residence, NJ. Custom home. 4. Contemporary lines are "softened" with traditional touches: exposed beams, glass door cabinets and extensive use of tile. Newsome residence, VT. Customized Arbor Place plan. ◐ 98. OPPOSITE: Layout and materials make a kitchen's major design statement; plan for both to endure — both functionally and aesthetically. 5. Custom residence, CA. Casa Carolina plan. ◐ 65. 6. Powelson residence, NJ. Customized Springfield plan. ◐ 112. 7. Pacific National Exhibition, BC. Custom home. 8. Vaucher Residence, OR. Customized Contempo Prow Star.

23

Pleasures of the Bath

Today's best bathrooms are an alluring combination of practical design and pampering amenities. With two or three bathrooms in most new homes, it's increasingly popular to transform one of them into a tranquil, spa-like retreat. Make it a personal haven where you can leave the world behind and soak up an environment that restores your energy and delights your senses. Good design is essential to making the most of any bath. So is being aware of your budget; costs per square foot tend to run higher in this room than any other.

➤ Plan plenty of storage for grooming accessories, towels and bath supplies.

➤ If possible, be lavish with windows to maximize the sense of space and natural light. How about a Lindal SkyWall over the tub? A garden window for growing your own herbal aromatherapies? Or a full sunroom for a bath as beautiful as all outdoors?

➤ Plan for amenities that will transform your bath into a private spa: a whirlpool tub, separate shower, multiple shower heads, a second sink, a sit-down vanity — and, again, plenty of storage.

➤ Bring your favorite music into your bath; tuck hidden stereo speakers into your plans.

➤ Use mirrors to expand small spaces.

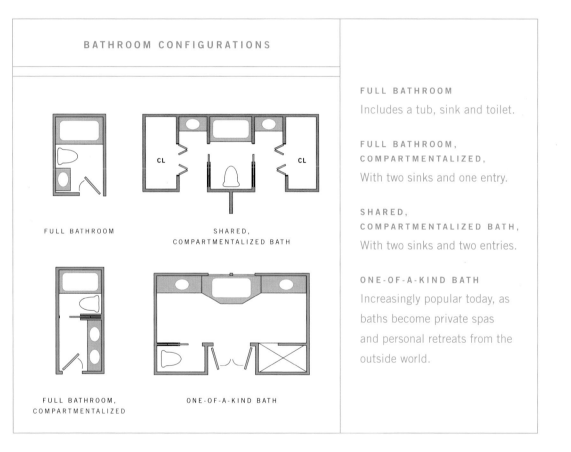

BATHROOM CONFIGURATIONS

FULL BATHROOM

SHARED, COMPARTMENTALIZED BATH

CL

CL

FULL BATHROOM, COMPARTMENTALIZED

ONE-OF-A-KIND BATH

FULL BATHROOM
Includes a tub, sink and toilet.

FULL BATHROOM, COMPARTMENTALIZED,
With two sinks and one entry.

SHARED, COMPARTMENTALIZED BATH,
With two sinks and two entries.

ONE-OF-A-KIND BATH
Increasingly popular today, as baths become private spas and personal retreats from the outside world.

25

➤ Double the useability of a bath by adding privacy walls or doors between fixtures. Two people can comfortably share a compartmentalized bath at the same time — a real blessing on busy mornings.

➤ Whenever possible, locate bathrooms on outside walls to take advantage of natural light and ventilation. You can also use a skylight; ventilating skylights are both beautiful and functional.

OPPOSITE An easy, eclectic mix of traditional and contemporary elements makes a personal statement of style. Lindal cedar ceiling liner complements the hardwood floor and adds warmth to this bath in Idaho's snow country. Hurlbutt residence, ID. Custom Pole.

OPPOSITE: 1. It's amazing what a well-placed window and mirror can do to expand the light and sense of space in a bathroom. Enger residence, WA. Custom home. 2. This large, luxurious custom bath makes dramatic use of marble. Digh residence, NC. Casa Islena Plan. ⊘ 67. 3. Glass blocks let in light without sacrificing privacy. Wiking residence, ID. Customized Casa. THIS PAGE: Custom bath designs and optional materials are often incorporated in Lindal homes — fróm frosted glass and real hot tubs to separate glass-enclosed showers and SunWalls. 4. Boyle residence, VA. Lakefront Living Plan. ◑ 105. 5. Wirtzfeld residence, HI. Custom home. 6. Freeman residence, MI. Custom home. 7. Cryer residence, HI. Custom home. 8. A Lindal SunRoom transforms a bath with a private outlook into a light-filled spa retreat; an adjacent window adds natural ventilation. Porter residence, Ontario. Customized Contempo Prow Star.

The Suite Life

Today's master suite goes beyond the bedroom to feature all the appointments of a private retreat. Many include a comfortable sitting area for reading and relaxing. Master baths are bigger than ever; often the most luxurious bath in the house is found here. A walk-in closet, built-in storage and dedicated dressing area can be elegantly designed into your plans. Capture views with windows or, better yet, sliding glass doors that open to a romantic garden or deck. Carefully consider furniture placement; queen- and king-sized beds consume lots of space. Plan ahead for television cabinetry, lighting needs

and hidden stereo speakers — special touches that are easy to incorporate now for years of enjoyment. When it comes to resale value, first-floor master suites are in high demand.

➤ Consider locating your master suite so that you can begin each day by waking up to sunlight and a wonderful view.

➤ Conversely, choose window coverings that allow you to shut out light when it's unwanted.

➤ To create an elegant, *en suite* look for your master bedroom and bath, use the same wall and floor coverings in both rooms — or at least stay true to the same color scheme. Look for ways to create a smooth visual transition.

➤ With a relatively small addition of square feet, you can create room for a quiet reading area in your master suite.

➤ Window seats are a lovely addition to any bedroom — romantic, functional and a charming focal point.

➤ Walk-in closets are big — in every way. Master suite closet systems are popular, tailor-made by space planners with their client's needs in mind. Built-in drawers can eliminate the need for stand-alone dressers and bring together your entire wardrobe in one convenient place. Some walk-in closets also incorporate, or open onto, a dressing area with ample mirrors and good lighting.

➤ Astral glass, and other types of clerestory windows, are popular in master suites; used to let in light from above, while protecting your privacy.

THIS PAGE: 1. Softly draped sliding glass doors open onto a deck off the master suite of this Lindal home. Leagjeld residence, OR. Customized designer. 2. The high ceilings and open floorplan of this modern master suite enhance its light, spacious look. Schutz residence, Ontario. Custom home. OPPOSITE: 3. Curtains below, unadorned windows above give this suite both privacy and natural light. Pacific National Exhibition, BC. Custom home. 4. Elegant country style is at home in this guest bedroom. Lindsey residence, KS. Customized Sienna Prairie. ☺ 61. 5. A gabled roof creates the focal point of this master suite. Pacific National Exhibition, BC. Custom home. 6. Astral glass lets in light high above the lofty bed. Lindsey residence, KS. Customized Sienna Prairie. ☺ 61.

Home Offices that Work

As more people are telecommuting, at least some of the time, the home office has become one of the fastest-growing trends in residential design. If you plan to work out of your home on a full-time basis now or in the future, chances are you'll want a dedicated office space. But many homeowners choose to combine a home office and a guest suite in one versatile room. Make it a self-sufficient space that allows privacy and quiet — whether it's for working or relaxing. A location just off the main entry or a separate entrance is ideal; so is a private bath. Plan electrical outlets and wiring to support your needs for good lighting, computer technology and high-speed telecommunications.

1. A wall of windows fill this home office with soft light; a swinging patio door opens onto a deck and an inspiring view. South residence, NJ. Customized Panorama. 2. Custom residence, NY. Chapel Hill plan. ◑ 93. 3. No need to devote an entire room to an office; here an area rug helps to carve out a small office within a larger room. Pacific National Exhibition, BC. Custom home. 4. Interior French doors make an elegant entrance to this office. Kling residence, ID. Ridgetop Ranch plan. ◑ 81.

Media Rooms

Big-screen televisions, VCRs or DVDs, stereo systems with surround sound — the technology that can be a wire-infested eyesore in an unplanned space comes together in high impact style when a room is designed to accommodate it. A media room makes great sense as a way to unite entertainment technologies and activities into one space. Situate your media room in the "public" part of your home, away from bedrooms and other spaces where privacy and quiet are important. Consider wiring, lighting, acoustics, built-in cabinetry and comfortable seating for a home theater that will get rave reviews.

1. A second-floor media room provides a private, relaxing space for family gatherings around games and TV. Pacific National Exhibition, BC. Custom home. 2. The pleasures of home entertainment are designed right into the living room of this home, with its custom-built shelves and storage, cedar ceiling and impressive stone fireplace. Hurlbutt residence, ID. Custom Pole. 3. A room totally dedicated to home entertainment, with custom electric curtains that black out window light, a semi-circular couch for comfortable viewing, and wiring to accommodate state-of-the-art technology. Chapman residence, MI. Customized Prow Star.

The Magic of Windows

"I WOULD NEVER HESITATE TO RECOMMEND LINDAL WINDOWS. MY EXPERIENCES WITH THEM AS A HOMEOWNER, CONTRACTOR AND DESIGNER HAVE ALL BEEN EXCELLENT."

— Roger MacPherson, Issaquah, Washington

Designing with windows is a balancing act of light, view, ventilation, energy efficiency and aesthetics. Lindal windows give you the best of all worlds — a combination of poetry and practicality that enhances the architectural character and sensory delights of your home. Open up your home to the charm of a garden or the calm of a water view. "Paint" your rooms with ever-changing natural light from sunrise to sunset. Circulate fresh air throughout your living spaces. The Lindal difference is in our combination of beauty and practicality — bringing together the finest materials and craftsmanship with sophisticated engineering, low maintenance and lasting energy efficiency.

➤ Decide what you want to achieve, both functionally and aesthetically, with the windows in your home. Where do you want privacy? A view? Where is ventilation important?

➤ The most appealing, balanced room lighting comes from windows on two walls.

➤ Windows have enormous impact on the energy efficiency of your home. For expertise and assistance in making the best choices in window frames, glazing and design, see your local Lindal dealer.

➤ Think about the visual impact of each window on the interior and exterior of your home.

➤ Stay true to a pattern of window style and placement that feels balanced.

➤ Consider the character of light. Northern light is diffused, but north-facing windows are energy drains in the winter. Eastern light is soft and pleasing. Southern light fuels passive solar gains — but plan for protection when heat comes on strong. Western light brings sunsets your way, but glare needs to be controlled in summer.

➤ And, Lindal has the best window warranty in the business. Ask your dealer for details.

THIS PAGE: 1. A softly arched custom window makes an architectural statement in a stairwell and illuminates it with soft light. Enger residence, WA. Custom home. 2. A succession of long, narrow skylights adds a sculptural quality of light to a loft hallway. Custom residence, BC. Custom home. OPPOSITE The fixed-glass windows of this Hawaii home are topped with jalousies — glass louvers that open to ventilate the room with cool trade winds. Custom residence, HI. Custom home.

Sunroom Style

"OUR SUNROOM IS OF EXCEPTIONAL QUALITY. IT ADDS GREAT BEAUTY AND ENJOYMENT FROM SUNRISE TO SUNSET."

— *Greg & Lydia LaHaie, Hillsboro, Oregon*

Does your dream home feature a light-filled two-story sunroom that reaches to the sky? A sun-drenched space off the kitchen where friends and family can relax? It's no wonder so many homeowners say their Lindal SunRoom is the most popular room in the house — all year round. We specialize in sunrooms whose elegant looks, quality craftsmanship and sophisticated engineering become an integral and inviting part of home — an enchanting place to greet the sun, gaze at the stars or catch a few quiet moments in between. And Lindal SunRooms are just the beginning; we offer a wide array of the most enlightened options under the sun.

➤ Whether you're remodeling an existing space or creating a new one, Lindal has a sunroom solution.

➤ A Solid Cedar SunRoom enhances the quality of your entire home — and the quality of life. It makes a great addition anytime.

➤ Another cost-effective alternative to a sunroom is a GardenRoom or PatioRoom. Custom designed to your specific needs, the choices are virtually limitless.

➤ A Lindal SkyWall is a perfect way to add drama and panoramic views to any kitchen or bathroom.

➤ A Lindal SunCanopy provides a bright, airy covered patio for outside entertaining.

➤ Lindal is the leading expert in designing a custom sunroom to fit your needs — whatever your style or budget.

OPPOSITE: A three-bay Lindal SunRoom creates a flourishing, light-bathed plant room as part of an enclosed passage between the garage and the home. Janssen residence, WA. Custom SunRoom. THIS PAGE: 1. A four-bay Lindal SunRoom surrounds double doors at the main entry, creating a gracious transition from exterior to interior. Frankos residence, MD. Custom home. 2. A custom Lindal SunCanopy turns an ordinary patio into a major design statement and a popular outdoor living space. Custom residence, CT. Customized SunCanopy. 3. A Lindal Patio Room is like a giant year-round sunroom without overhead glass; this one encloses the family spa. Cronie residence, WA. Customized GardenRoom.

THIS PAGE: 1. There's a dramatic difference between a sunroom that looks like a tacked-on afterthought and this Lindal SunRoom, which is elegantly at home with the building materials and architectural style. Tillotson residence, WA. Custom SunRoom. OPPOSITE 2. A straight-eave Lindal SunRoom adds space and soft Northern light to an informal dining area off the kitchen. Bohnenberger residence, SC. Custom SunRoom. 3. A Lindal SkyWall highlights the panoramic view from this kitchen. Scott residence, WA. Custom SkyWall. 4. A Lindal SkyWall looks out to a glorious water view from this master suite. Overhead glass encloses special gases between double panes for extra sun protection. Lindal residence, WA. Custom SunRoom. 5. A custom corner-sunroom from Lindal creates a dining room with the ambiance of a glass-enclosed conservatory. Custom residence, MI. Custom SunRoom.

Lighting Design

Often neglected in the design and building of most homes, the impact of good lighting design illuminates many of today's finest custom interiors. Artful, functional lighting can do so much to enhance the comfort and aesthetic appeal of your home that it's worth some careful planning. In the last few years, innovative technology has multiplied the options. Do some research and define your needs early

on, when it's easiest and least expensive to wire your home and install fixtures accordingly. A little enlightened thinking now will add pleasure, functionality and value to the life of your home.

➤ Consider the character of light you want in various areas of your home. Wall sconces provide upward light, which is soft and indirect — wonderful mood lighting. Recessed and track lighting focus downward directly on a surface or object — great for illuminating a painting or any area that calls for a spotlight. Careful aim is critical to keep these lights from creating glare and shining into eyes; diffusers can help. Table lamps are ideal for task lighting and the plug-in mobility they provide. Cove lighting adds indirect light behind a molding around the ceiling of a room.

➤ Keep your fixtures in sync with the architectural style and interior decor of your home. Consider other fixtures and light sources in the room — including windows and skylights.

➤ Track lighting is more sophisticated and versatile than ever; choose the type of light bulbs

and overall scale that best complement your decor and functional needs.

➤ Choose bulbs that create the quality of light you want. Energy-efficient fluorescent bulbs produce cool, diffuse light; today's choices are a world away from the flickering bluish flourescents of the past. Halogens provide strong, direct illumination that's closer to daylight. Miniature halogen bulbs are popular as art and accent lighting.

➤ Nothing lets you alter the mood in a room more quickly than a dimmer switch.

THIS PAGE: 1. An appealing mix of functional and ambient lighting: adjustable track lighting, task lighting over the island, and built-in lighting below the cabinets on either side of the sink. Hodgkinson residence, Ontario. Customized Ellington plan. ❷ 107. 2. Recessed ceiling light is unobtrusive and easily controlled with dimmer switches. Abbatiello residence, SC. Custom home. 3. Built-in ambient lighting is tucked behind a beam by the fireplace; floor lamps provide comfortable reading light on either side. Bear Creek Lodge, ID. Commercial Lodge.

Life Without Barriers

A living environment that works means different things at different times of life. With a little forethought now, you can ensure that you'll never be forced into a move later on because your home is no longer accessible to you. Designing homes without limits applies "barrier-free" thinking to the practicalities of getting around the house in a wheelchair. The added effort and expense are minimal when you incorporate these design considerations into your home plans from the start. It's a small price for a home that will last you a lifetime.

CONTEMPO PROW STAR

OceanSide

BEDROOMS three

BATHROOMS 2 full

MASTER BEDROOM first floor

TOTAL AREA 2,177 sq. ft.

FIRST FLOOR 2,177 sq. ft.

SIZE 68' x 38'

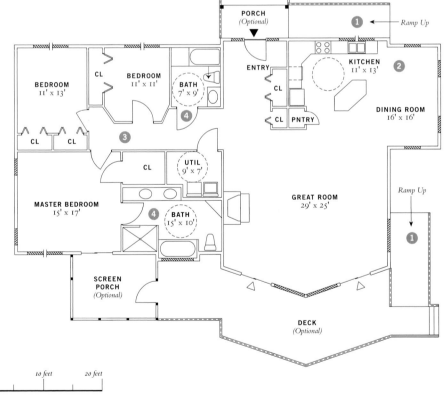

0 feet   10 feet   20 feet

⅟₁₆ inch represents 1 foot

1 When possible, eliminate stairs from your plans; outside, use gently sloped ramps for above grade entries, inside, opt for one-level living. **2** Kitchen counters and equipment should be within easy reach. Use lever-action door handles throughout the house instead of doorknobs. **3** Expand the width of your halls to at least 40 inches; doorways to 36 inches. **4** Increase the overall size of your bathrooms to easily accommodate the 5 foot turning radius of a wheelchair. Reinforce walls now to allow for grab bars later.

Outdoor Living

"LIVING IN OUR LINDAL IS LIKE BEING ON VACATION EVERY DAY."

— David & Cathy Osterman, Cumberland Cove, Tennessee

You gain a lot more than square feet when you extend your living space outdoors with a deck or covered porch. These are the places memories are made — where leisurely days and starlit nights are spent relaxing and entertaining. Lindal decks combine top-quality materials with a superb building system, so there's none of the squeaking or bouncing so common in lesser-built options. Your deck can be designed in any size or configuration that enhances your site and your outdoor activities.

➤ For the ultimate in beauty and practicality, choose decking, railing and framing in Western red cedar. It resists rot and insects.

➤ Sliding glass or patio doors make it a breeze to serve meals outdoors.

➤ Plan ahead for a hot tub. Decide where it will be located and add reinforcement, support and plumbing below the deck according to the tub manufacturer's instructions.

➤ Multi-level decks can provide separate areas of activity and visual interest.

➤ Consider built-in seating and large planters as part of your deck design.

➤ Sturdy railings add a finished look to your outdoor living space. For safety, be sure to build railings according to local codes and to Lindal specifications.

➤ A screened-in porch is a welcome oasis in hot climates where you want to let in cool breezes and keep out insects.

➤ At night, lighting can turn a deck into a romantic outdoor haven. It's an important safety consideration, too.

OPPOSITE Extend your living space outdoors with a covered porch or deck. Custom residence, NY. Chapel Hill plan. ❶ 93. THIS PAGE: 1. This home's design for entertaining continues outdoors with a large, two-level deck that leads to the lakefront yard and boat dock. Chapman residence, MI. Customized Prow Star. 2. The optional wider boards used here are especially attractive when you're decking a lot of square feet. Gassner residence, OR. Octagon Oasis plan. ❷ 110. 3. A deck of Lindal cedar surrounds a swimming pool overlooking Maui; a glass railing provides wind protection without blocking the view. Barnette residence, HI. Customized Prow Star.

41

03

Once you have a clear picture of your home's architectural style and floorplan, you're ready to make other major choices that distinguish the quality and beauty of your Lindal home. Your local dealer is well-versed in every aspect of these options and many more, so don't hesitate to get an expert's insight as you choose your Lindal siding, roofing, insulation and other premium Lindal home products. Isn't it good to know that whatever choices you make, you can count on Lindal for superior engineering, craftsmanship and materials? It's all a matter of your preferences and priorities.

Doors

The doors in your home are a highly personal choice. Style is always a concern, especially at the main entrance. Be sure to think about security and energy efficiency as well as good looks. We have. Lindal's standard entry door is made of galvanized steel with a polyurethane core, and a wide variety of wood and custom-crafted doors are available as options. Inside, our premium doors give you the strength and noise insulation of solid wood. Consider Lindal glass doors wherever you would like to make a magical transition between rooms — or to the outdoors.

CUSTOM SOLID WOOD ENTRY DOOR

GLASS PANEL DOOR

CUSTOM SOLID WOOD ENTRY DOOR

STANDARD STEEL ENTRY DOOR

SOLID-CORE INTERIOR DOOR

LINDAL DOORS Never underestimate the impact of a Lindal door. The styles above are only a sample of the dozens of Lindal doors available that add character, quality and value to every room in your house. Your Lindal dealer can help you choose the perfect Lindal doors — even draw on other custom sources to get the style and materials you're looking for.

Siding

Finish your home's exterior with your choice of Lindal's wide selection of siding styles in premium Western red cedar. You'll find the perfect exterior finish to enhance the architectural style and natural surroundings of your home. You can combine several finishes — for example, cedar shingles and clapboard — or accent the beauty of the wood with stone, brick, or stucco. Lindal's premium grade of select, tight-knot Western red cedar makes for long, attractive siding — a dramatic difference from today's typical short lengths that come from cutting defects out of lower-grade lumber. Lindal cedar has no loose or missing knots, and is available in a wide array of pre-stained siding colors.

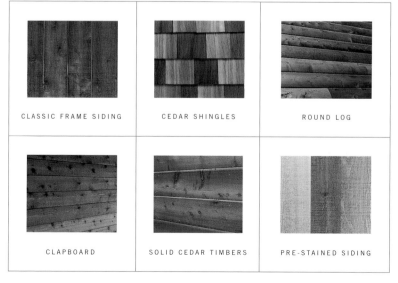

CLASSIC FRAME SIDING   CEDAR SHINGLES   ROUND LOG

CLAPBOARD   SOLID CEDAR TIMBERS   PRE-STAINED SIDING

Insulation

Now's the time to plan for an energy-efficient home. It's not costly to add extra insulation when you build — but it's an expensive hassle later on. Because more heat escapes from the roof than from the walls of your home, the roof is the first and best place to add extra insulation. In cold climates, consider adding extra insulation to walls and floors. Lindal offers insulation packages that keep our homes cozy and energy-efficient in any climate. For warm, humid climates, Lindal's tropical roof is designed to be open with circulation in mind. Your local Lindal dealer can help you determine your insulation needs based on the design of your roof, the temperatures, wind and snow loads of your location.

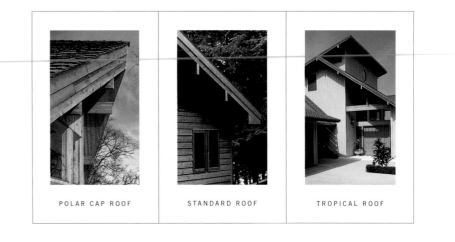

POLAR CAP ROOF   STANDARD ROOF   TROPICAL ROOF

Roofs

Lindal's engineered roof system gives you a lifetime of strength, energy efficiency — and the flexibility to match the style, pitch and roofing materials to your home's architecture. If you live in a cold climate, consider our Polar Cap options; they add extra insulation to our standard roof system. Whatever Lindal roof system you choose, you can count on excellent ventilation — thanks to continuous vents that run the entire length of the soffit and ridge. Together, they create a continuous air flow that keeps roof framing and insulation dry, preventing the moisture that can cause rot and mold. The same system also channels out unwanted heat in summer, which can help reduce the need for air conditioning.

HAND-SPLIT CEDAR SHAKES: A DELUXE OPTION

OPTIONAL SHAKE ROOF

COMPOSITE SHINGLES

OPTIONAL DECRA ROOFING

LINDAL ROOFS Lindal's #1 grade composite roof shingles come with a 25-year guarantee. Cedar shakes are a popular custom option, as are the new generation of materials that combine the look of a shake roof with the durability of highly-technology finishes.

Windows

Built like fine furniture, Lindal windows are available in a wide array of styles and custom sizes that enhance the architectural style of your home. Beyond their sheer beauty, you'll find the highest industry rating for their ability to prevent air and water infiltration under the toughest test conditions. State-of-the-art Low E Argon glass is our standard for comfort, energy efficiency and reduced fading of draperies and furniture fabrics. And it comes with a lifetime guarantee. Lindal windows are available with premium grade clear cedar or vinyl frames inside and out — or with the best of both worlds: optional low maintenance vinyl outside, warm cedar inside.

AWNING WINDOW

CASEMENT WINDOW

VINYL WINDOW

CUSTOM FIXED WINDOW

FIXED WINDOW

GARDEN WINDOW

Decks

When it comes to outdoor living, nothing beats the lasting pleasures and aesthetic appeal of a Lindal deck. From a multi-level outdoor living room with built-in seating and a hot tub to a sunny balcony off a second-floor bedroom or bath, you can count on Lindal's renowned quality and craftsmanship. That's important, because bouncy, squeaky decks built of 1-inch boards are common even in custom homes. But Lindal decks are strong and silent, thanks to our select, tight-knot 2-inch-thick cedar decking and 2 x 8 or larger framing — the best in the industry. And our decking is finished on all four sides, with rounded edges that prevent splintering.

Your local Lindal dealer has the technical and design know-how to create decks that are fine-tuned to your needs and the architectural character of your home.

CUSTOM DECK AND RAIL

STANDARD 2 X 2 LINDAL RAIL

STANDARD 2 X 4 LINDAL DECKING

LINDAL DECKS: ABOVE LEFT A roomy wrap-around deck with deep overhangs creates an exotic outdoor living space. Optional peeled-log posts, a finely crafted railing and extra-wide deck boards reflect the tropical setting. ABOVE RIGHT The beauty of a standard Lindal deck rail: 2 x 2 cedar verticals crowned with a 2 x 4 top rail. LOWER RIGHT When it comes to making a meal or any moment seem special, there's nothing like an expansive deck for entertaining.

Variations on a Theme

You almost have to see it to believe what an impact a few fairly simple modifications can make to the style of your home.

Some changes are as simple as your choice of exterior materials, or the addition of accent materials, to reflect your tastes and your home's setting. Shingles have made a comeback as a popular exterior accent with timeless appeal. Combinations of cedar, stucco and/or brick lend added interest to the exterior of large homes and emphasize architectural focal points.

A change in the shape or placement of windows can enhance or alter the character of your home's "personality" and give it an entirely different architectural look. The opportunities — and results — are especially dramatic when your home design includes a Lindal prow. As the illustrations on this page reveal, a prow gives you the flexibility to create just the look you want by playing with the shape, size and number of windows, by adding architectural elements such as a bay or decorative elements such as a truss.

Your local Lindal dealer is an expert in helping to explore the many ways that such minor modifications can create a tremendous visual impact. Meanwhile, take a look at just a few of the ways you can modify your Lindal home to create a timeless style. This is one time in life when change is easy.

50

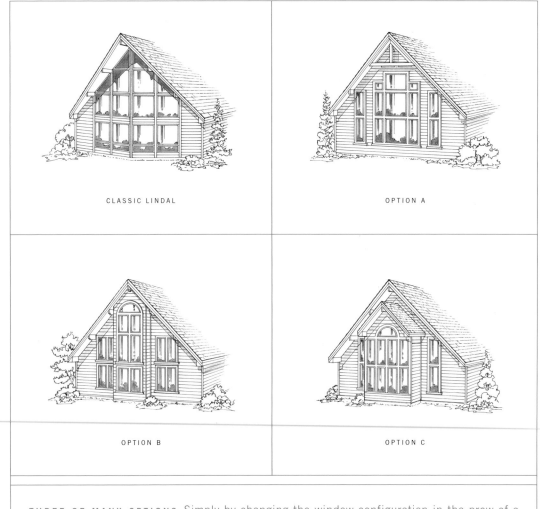

CLASSIC LINDAL

OPTION A

OPTION B

OPTION C

THREE OF MANY OPTIONS Simply by changing the window configuration in the prow of a Lindal design, you can create very different exterior looks — from classic to contemporary to traditional. Your local Lindal dealer can help you explore the wide range of possibilities.

CRAFTSMAN

SOUTHWEST

RUSTIC WITH ROUND LOG SIDING

SAME HOME, COMPLETELY DIFFERENT LOOKS Take a look at what a difference windows, exterior siding and entry style can make. **TOP** A decorative truss — covered entry and shingle siding with stucco. **MIDDLE** A stucco exterior, tile roof and more formal covered entry. **BOTTOM** Round log siding with a rustic-looking covered entry. Reference ℗ 99 for the full floorplan shown above.

Your Building System

"THE FLEXIBILITY OF LINDAL'S BUILDING SYSTEM IS JUST INCREDIBLE."

— Tom & Sue Button, Washington

Not many custom homes give you a choice of building systems. Lindal homes do. Inspired by North American masterbuilders, our classic post and beam building system is the cornerstone of Lindal's signature style and longstanding reputation. We also offer a conventionally framed building system, designed to save you money without sacrificing quality. This is the system commonly used in the construction industry today. But there's nothing common about the materials or craftsmanship that go into either Lindal building system. Both feature superior-grade, kiln-dried Lindal cedar and an attention to detail uncommon in home building today.

The vast majority of Lindal home designs can be constructed in either building system — so the choice is truly yours, and your local Lindal dealer can help you decide.

LINDAL CLASSIC POST AND BEAM

Lindal's signature building system uses a strong framework of posts and beams to support the roof's weight. This frees up most interior walls from serving as structural supports. The result is an open, airy interior that allows long spans, soaring ceilings, large expanses of glass — and the design flexibility to customize any floorplan to suit your functional and aesthetic tastes. Exposed beams showcase the beauty of Lindal materials.

LINDAL CONVENTIONALLY FRAMED

Lindal's conventionally framed building system is similar to the truss or rafter framework of most home construction — with one dramatic

difference: Lindal quality. This building system is ideal if you value cozier interior spaces and significant savings on material costs. Even labor costs can be lower. With some additional engineering, many of our classic Lindal designs can be "translated" into our conventionally framed building system — saving you money without sacrificing Lindal quality or style.

LEFT Lindal's popular Summit style features large expanses of glass and a cathedral great room — two hallmarks of Lindal's post and beam building system. Wadsworth Residence, MI. Customized Summit. RIGHT Equally at home in town or country settings, Lindal's conventional building system provide plenty of design choices and cost efficiencies, too. Both building systems are covered by Lindal's Lifetime Structural Warranty. Skala Residence, SC. Custom home.

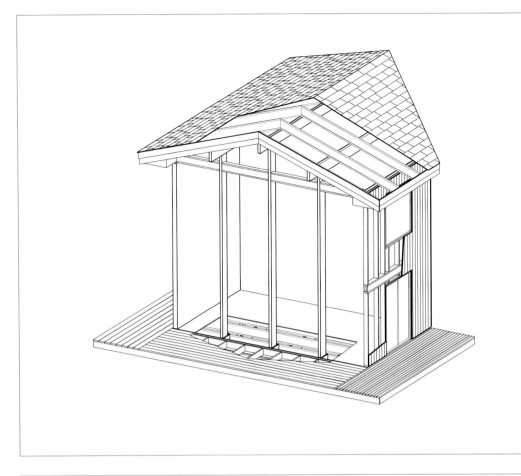

CLASSIC POST AND BEAM

➤ A strong framework of posts and beams support the roof's weight.

➤ Interior walls are usually freed from serving as structural support.

➤ Allows for an open, airy interior with high ceilings.

➤ Supports long spans and large expanses of glass.

➤ Provides exceptional design flexibility.

➤ Inspired by North American masterbuilders.

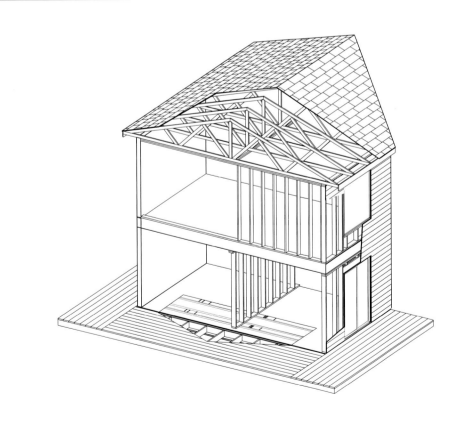

CONVENTIONAL FRAMING

➤ The building system similar to that used by many residential builders.

➤ Walls generally bear the load of the roof.

➤ Often provides lower construction and materials costs.

➤ Choose from truss or rafter roof systems. Rafter roofs open up the interior and can allow for soaring ceilings; conventional truss roofs create intimate spaces with lower ceilings.

➤ Conventional framing, Lindal quality.

The Lindal Process

"WE HAVE BOTH COMPARED THE LINDAL METHOD OF CONSTRUCTION WITH THAT OF OTHER HOUSES BEING CUSTOM-BUILT IN OUR NEIGHBORHOOD, AND WE ARE GLAD WE CHOSE LINDAL"

— *Derek & Candy Stott, Ontario*

54

How long will it take? What will it cost? Naturally, the answers to schedule and budget vary with each homeowner's priorities and plans. Once you have a preliminary plan on paper, your local Lindal dealer can provide a cost estimate and delivery schedule. Of course, construction schedules are determined by your builder. But there are dozens of things we do to expedite construction and ensure that your Lindal home is the best building experience and custom home value on the market today, and tomorrow.

BUDGET-WISE THINKING

Building a Lindal gives you an unbeatable level of control over where you put your money. For example, if you're buying a lot with a knockout view, you'll probably devote a significant percentage of your budget to the property itself. And finishing costs differ dramatically; obviously, granite counters cost more than laminate, a whirlpool bathtub more than a standard one.

Which brings us to an important reminder as you develop a budget: Your Lindal is only part of the package. Be sure to include the cost of your property, excavation, landscaping, construction and interior finishing such as carpet, fixtures and cabinetry.

Other factors that will affect total costs: your site and the ease of building on it; the size and design of your home (two-story homes tend to cost less per square foot than one-story homes); construction costs, which vary with location and complexity; and whether you plan to put any "sweat equity" into building your home.

Your local independent Lindal dealer can be a great help in making the most of your budget — advising where your dollars should go to get the most home for your money and providing ballpark estimates for construction in your area.

QUALITY AND COST

When you compare cost, don't forget to compare quality. "Settling for less" can easily wind up costing more in the long run. Ask any and all competitive bidders to base their prices on Lindal's standard materials — same quantity, same quality (when they can get it). Year after year, our homeowners tell us they got more home for their money. Value is the Lindal difference.

COMPARING APPLES TO APPLES

If you've been shopping around, you may have been told that you can get the same impeccable quality of a Lindal for a lower bottom line. But are you getting the information you need to make an apples-to-apples comparison? Make sure you also consider architectural design costs, structural warranties, and assistance in siting, framing, and designing your dream home.

OPPOSITE PAGE The basic process that many of you will follow while designing and building your Lindal dream home. Some changes to the process may occur, however, due to local building requirements and the complexity of the home you wish to build. Your local Lindal Dealer will be happy to review this process with you and determine a process that is particular to your personal needs.

01 PLANNING:
DETERMINE A BUDGET

Visit a mortgage company to pre-qualify or, based on your income and savings, determine what you're prepared to spend. Your local Lindal dealer can help you design a home that's within your budget.

02 PLANNING:
SELECT A FLOORPLAN

Your dealer can help choose the plan closest in design and rough cost to what you have in mind. It's important to find a building lot before the actual design of your home. Lindal can custom-design a home for a small additional fee.

03 PLANNING:
BUILDING SITE

If you already have your building lot, your local Lindal dealer can analyze it for you — helping to adapt your design to the site to minimize dramatic topographical changes, which can be costly.

04 PLANNING:
PRICING

Once your home has been designed and modified to suit your needs, your Lindal designer can complete a preliminary price on the materials package for your home design.

05 ORDER & DESIGN:
HOME ORDER

When you're ready to proceed, you'll need to complete a full home order which includes a signed Purchase and Sale Agreement, a deposit with Lindal, and approved sketches. At this point, you are officially underway!

06 ORDER & DESIGN:
MORTGAGE LOAN

Immediately following the placement of your home order, it is vital to meet again with your mortgage company to begin both the construction loan and the long-term mortgage process.

07 ORDER & DESIGN:
DRAFTING SCHEDULE

The first stage of your home's drafting process is scheduled at Lindal. You are kept informed of this schedule by your local Lindal dealer.

08 ORDER & DESIGN:
DRAWINGS ARRIVE

You receive the Preliminary Plans for review; now's the time to make any additional changes. After they are approved, signed and returned to Lindal, Final Construction Drawings can be completed.

09 PRODUCTION:
BULIDING CONTRACTOR

With Construction Drawings in hand, you can begin selecting a building contractor and acquiring a building permit. Your Lindal consultant can help. These drawings will allow you to get complete bids from potential builders.

10 PRODUCTION:
SHIPPING SCHEDULE

Once you've arranged financing, chosen your builder and made sure the building site is accessible, you sign an authorization to place your order on the Lindal shipping schedule, and we begin putting your home together.

11 PRODUCTION:
FINAL PAYMENT

Prior to shipment of the home package, a final payment to Lindal must be received. Your mortgage company will handle this for you.

12 PRODUCTION:
FOUNDATION/PREPARATION

Your selected builder gets the foundation ready before the building materials arrive.

13 DELIVERY & CONSTRUCTION:
DELIVERY

The Lindal home package is delivered by truck to your building site, where the builder unloads the material and your Lindal dealer takes a complete materials inventory.

14 DELIVERY & CONSTRUCTION:
CONSTRUCTION

Your builder begins construction of the floor system, followed by posts, beams, rafters and roof sheathing. Next come the windows, siding and doors.

15 DELIVERY & CONSTRUCTION:
FINISHING

Plumbing, electrical, insulation, drywall, paneling, ceiling, walls and paint are completed. You select finishing items to be installed by your builder — including cabinets, appliances, fixtures, etc.

16 DELIVERY & CONSTRUCTION:
LANDSCAPING

To save money, some homeowners move into their homes and complete their own landscaping as time allows; others prefer to move into a completed home with landscaping in full bloom.

Get Your Plan on Paper

"WE CHOSE LINDAL CEDAR HOMES BECAUSE WE WANTED AN OPEN FLOORPLAN. THE KITCHEN, DINING ROOM AND LIVING ROOM ARE COMBINED INTO ONE LARGE GREAT ROOM."

— Dotty Kelley, Scotland, Connecticut

With the knowledge and insights gained from your Lifestyle Inventory on page 14, Lindal's home planning ideas, and your site plan, you can now either make an informed choice from the design library ahead, or create your home from scratch. We suggest using a trick of the architect's trade: Draw a bubble for every major living space — and watch your home's layout take shape as you arrange and rearrange them into a plan that works. For most people, getting their dream down on paper is one of the most exciting steps in building their Lindal — exceeded only, of course, by the finished results.

1. START WITH A BUBBLE DESIGN

Draw a bubble for each major living space and identify each with a letter ("K" for kitchen, "B" for bedroom, and so on). The size of each bubble should roughly represent the size of each room. Refer back to your responses on the square foot guide on page 15. Now have some fun with them. Make loose sketches, and don't worry about the accuracy of scale; the spatial relationships among rooms are what matter most now. Remember outside influences, such as views, to zero in on the ideal location for each room.

2. A LOOSE INTERPRETATION

Once you have a clear idea of how your rooms should interrelate, let the circles take the shape of actual rooms.

3. A LINE DRAWING

Now link the rooms in a preliminary line drawing of your floorplan. You can even include interior doorways, major windows, decks — as much detail as you have at this point.

and other amenities — whether it's a wine cellar, a piano or an entertainment center.

4. BRING SCALE INTO THE PICTURE

Discover how gratifying it is to bring your plan into scale; your Lindal dealer can produce a study drawing for you which will help bring your ideas into scale.

A scale drawing helps you determine whether your plan will work the way you want it to, as well as accommodate special furniture

CAN WE HELP?

You may enjoy the design process, but at any point along the way, you can turn to your local Lindal dealer for design support and a complimentary feasibility and cost analysis. Of course, you just may find your dream plan — or one that's close to it — in the design library ahead.

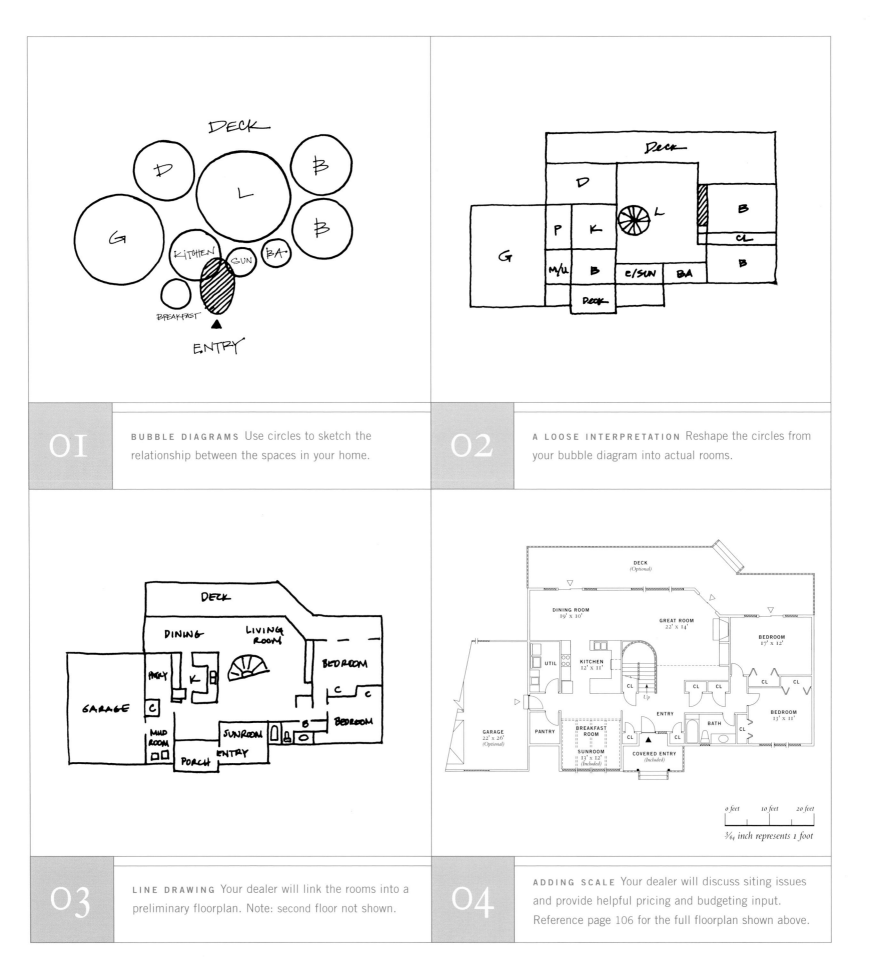

57

OI BUBBLE DIAGRAMS Use circles to sketch the relationship between the spaces in your home.

O2 A LOOSE INTERPRETATION Reshape the circles from your bubble diagram into actual rooms.

O3 LINE DRAWING Your dealer will link the rooms into a preliminary floorplan. Note: second floor not shown.

O4 ADDING SCALE Your dealer will discuss siting issues and provide helpful pricing and budgeting input. Reference page 106 for the full floorplan shown above.

04

Lindal home plans are the ultimate in livability and style — the culmination of decades of professional design and home-building experience. The following pages feature our latest home designs and updated versions of our all-time best-sellers. And these are only the beginning. At your local Lindal dealer, you'll find many more Lindal home designs along with the personal assistance to modify any plan you choose. Count on your local Lindal dealer anytime during the planning process, and whenever you'd like a complimentary feasibility and cost analysis of your plan. Or, if you prefer, just give your Lindal dealer your wish list — and let us do the work.

How to Read Plans

Available exclusively through Lindal and your local Lindal dealer, our collection of home plans is the ultimate in livability and style — the culmination of decades of design and home building experience. As you browse, keep in mind that it's easy for us to make modifications to your favorite plan and give you the best of both worlds: your own personal version of a proven design. Your local Lindal dealer can assist you at any time during your planning process, and whenever you'd like a complimentary feasibility and cost analysis of your plan.

➤ Photos sometimes show materials supplied by Lindal used differently than they are depicted in the authorized Lindal plans. Be sure to comply with your local building codes. Some options pictured in this book may not be available; see your local Lindal dealer for the complete selection of current options.

➤ Floorplans, photos and illustrations sometimes show features not supplied by Lindal, such as stucco, brick, decorative columns, and trusses, chimneys, fireplaces, appliances, fixtures, etc.

➤ Floorplans, photos and illustrations often show optional features not included in the base price — such as garages, decks, porches, skylights, sunrooms, custom windows, some trim packages, etc. These products are available from Lindal.

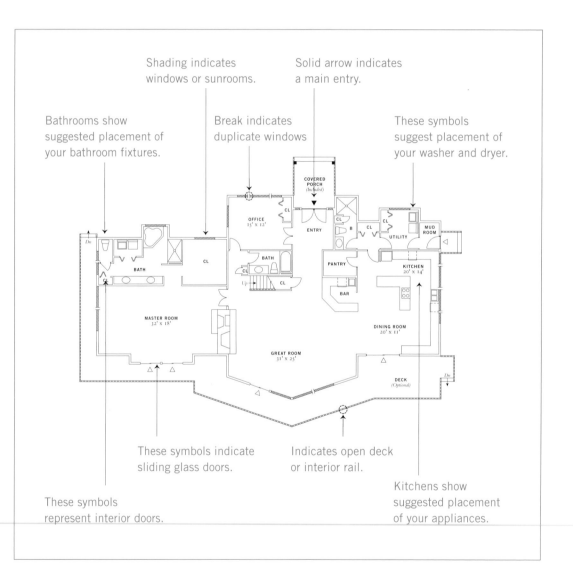

Shading indicates windows or sunrooms.

Solid arrow indicates a main entry.

Bathrooms show suggested placement of your bathroom fixtures.

Break indicates duplicate windows

These symbols suggest placement of your washer and dryer.

These symbols indicate sliding glass doors.

Indicates open deck or interior rail.

These symbols represent interior doors.

Kitchens show suggested placement of your appliances.

So when you're planning your home, it's imperative that you consult with the independent Lindal dealer nearest you. They know the local building codes and have the best resources to find any additional items you desire to make your house your own.

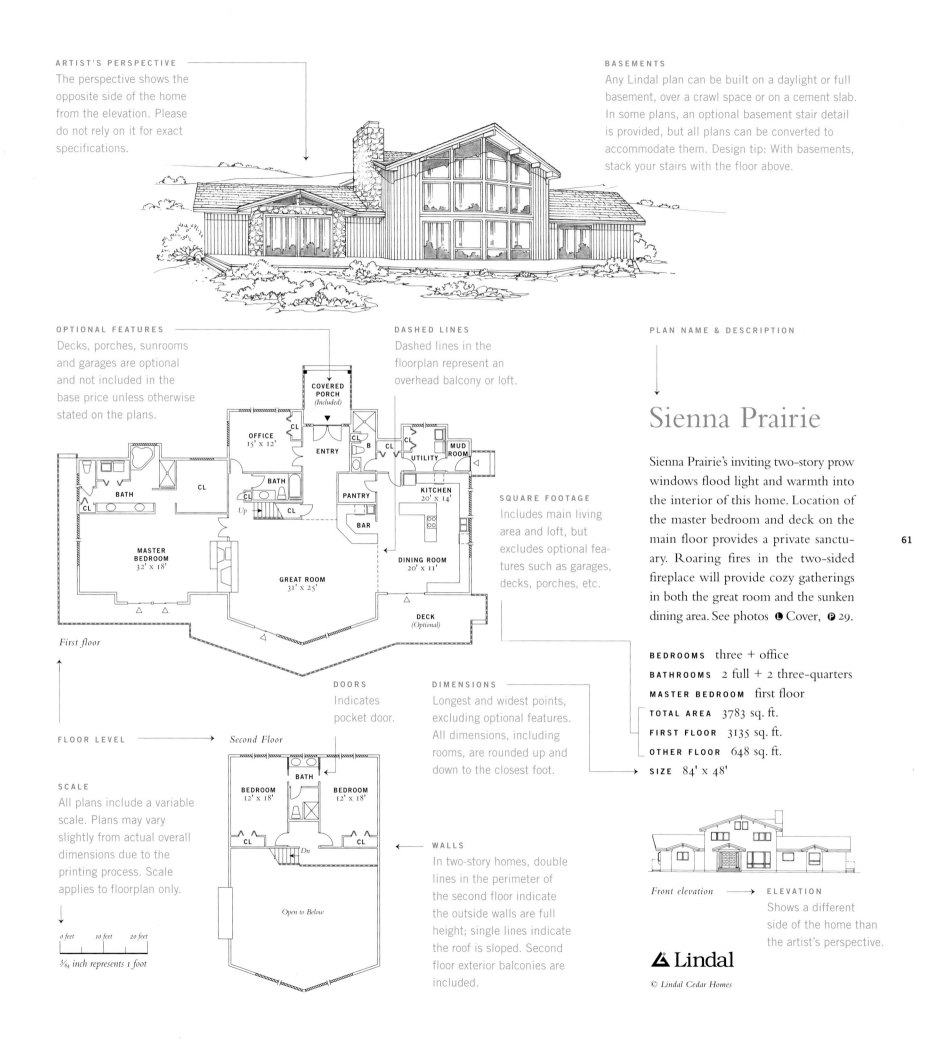

ARTIST'S PERSPECTIVE
The perspective shows the opposite side of the home from the elevation. Please do not rely on it for exact specifications.

BASEMENTS
Any Lindal plan can be built on a daylight or full basement, over a crawl space or on a cement slab. In some plans, an optional basement stair detail is provided, but all plans can be converted to accommodate them. Design tip: With basements, stack your stairs with the floor above.

OPTIONAL FEATURES
Decks, porches, sunrooms and garages are optional and not included in the base price unless otherwise stated on the plans.

DASHED LINES
Dashed lines in the floorplan represent an overhead balcony or loft.

PLAN NAME & DESCRIPTION

Sienna Prairie

Sienna Prairie's inviting two-story prow windows flood light and warmth into the interior of this home. Location of the master bedroom and deck on the main floor provides a private sanctuary. Roaring fires in the two-sided fireplace will provide cozy gatherings in both the great room and the sunken dining area. See photos ❶ Cover, ❷ 29.

61

BEDROOMS three + office
BATHROOMS 2 full + 2 three-quarters
MASTER BEDROOM first floor
TOTAL AREA 3783 sq. ft.
FIRST FLOOR 3135 sq. ft.
OTHER FLOOR 648 sq. ft.
SIZE 84' x 48'

First floor (floorplan labels)

COVERED PORCH *(Included)*
OFFICE 15' x 12'
ENTRY
CL / B / MUD ROOM / UTILITY
BATH
PANTRY
KITCHEN 20' x 14'
BAR
MASTER BEDROOM 32' x 18'
Up
GREAT ROOM 31' x 25'
DINING ROOM 20' x 11'
DECK *(Optional)*

First floor

SQUARE FOOTAGE
Includes main living area and loft, but excludes optional features such as garages, decks, porches, etc.

DOORS
Indicates pocket door.

DIMENSIONS
Longest and widest points, excluding optional features. All dimensions, including rooms, are rounded up and down to the closest foot.

FLOOR LEVEL

Second Floor

Second Floor (floorplan labels)

BATH
BEDROOM 12' x 18'
BEDROOM 12' x 18'
CL
CL
Dn
Open to Below

SCALE
All plans include a variable scale. Plans may vary slightly from actual overall dimensions due to the printing process. Scale applies to floorplan only.

0 feet   10 feet   20 feet

³⁄₆₄ inch represents 1 foot

WALLS
In two-story homes, double lines in the perimeter of the second floor indicate the outside walls are full height; single lines indicate the roof is sloped. Second floor exterior balconies are included.

Front elevation

ELEVATION
Shows a different side of the home than the artist's perspective.

⚠ Lindal

© Lindal Cedar Homes

Classic Lindal

Imagine panoramic prow fronts. Walls of windows. Vaulted ceilings graced with Western red cedar. A flow of interior space as luxurious as it is functional. These are the hallmarks of Classic Lindal design — as fresh and inviting today as it was 55 years ago. Classic Lindal elements of style are made possible by patented engineering strengths that allow for long, unobstructed spans and expanses of glass. The result is a diverse collection of some of the most appealing homes in residential design — a mix of casual elegance and livability that never goes out of style.

First floor

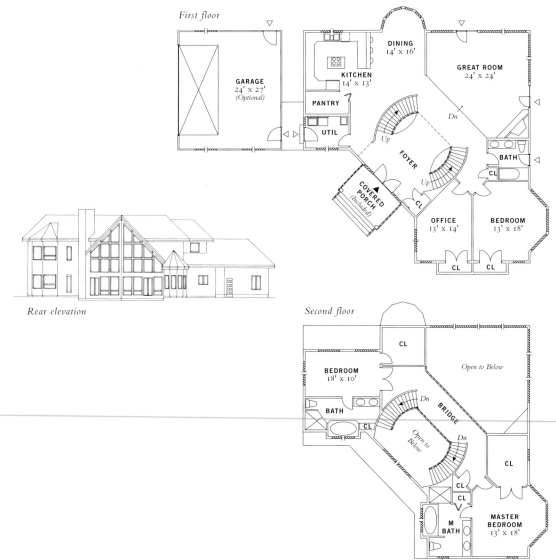

GARAGE
24' x 27'
(Optional)

DINING
14' x 16'

KITCHEN
14' x 13'

GREAT ROOM
24' x 24'

PANTRY

UTIL

Dn

FOYER

BATH

CL

COVERED
PORCH
(Included)

Up

Up

CL

OFFICE
13' x 14'

BEDROOM
13' x 18'

CL

CL

Rear elevation

Second floor

CL

BEDROOM
18' x 10'

Open to Below

BATH

CL

Dn

BRIDGE

Open to Below

Dn

CL

CL

CL

M
BATH

MASTER
BEDROOM
13' x 18'

Casa Angelina

A sense of traditional values permeates Casa Angelina with its bay windows adorning the dining room and second-floor master bedroom. Details such as gabled dormers and a multi-level roof add an architectural elegance. A dramatic semi-circular optional staircase leads from one floor to the other in unequaled style.

BEDROOMS three + office + media room

BATHROOMS 3 full

MASTER BEDROOM second floor

TOTAL AREA 3,456 sq. ft.

FIRST FLOOR 2,213 sq. ft.

OTHER FLOOR 1,243 sq. ft.

SIZE 53' x 60'

0 feet   10 feet   20 feet

3/64 inch represents 1 foot

Lindal

© Lindal Cedar Homes

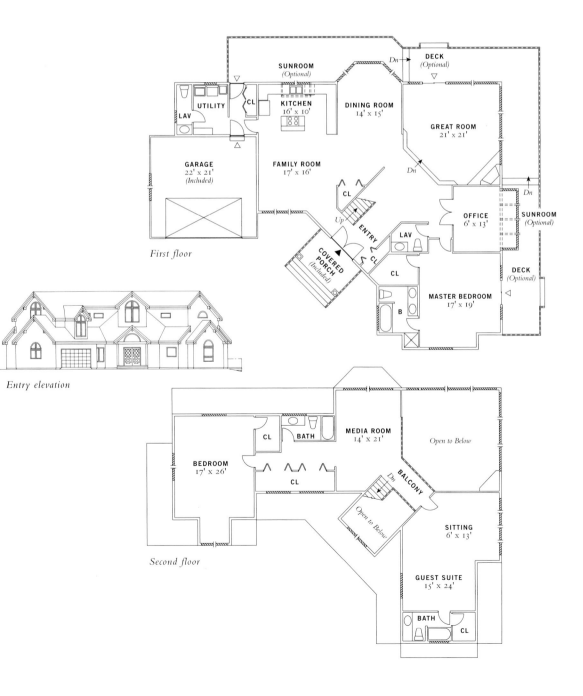

SUNROOM
(Optional)

DECK
(Optional)

Dn

UTILITY

LAV

CL

KITCHEN
16' x 10'

DINING ROOM
14' x 15'

GREAT ROOM
21' x 21'

GARAGE
22' x 21'
(Included)

FAMILY ROOM
17' x 16'

Dn

CL

Up

ENTRY

Dn

OFFICE
6' x 13'

SUNROOM
(Optional)

COVERED PORCH
(Included)

LAV

CL

CL

MASTER BEDROOM
17' x 19'

DECK
(Optional)

B

First floor

Entry elevation

BEDROOM
17' x 26'

CL

BATH

CL

MEDIA ROOM
14' x 21'

Open to Below

CL

BALCONY

Dn

Open to Below

SITTING
6' x 13'

GUEST SUITE
15' x 24'

Second floor

BATH

CL

Casa Carolina

The Casa Carolina lives up to its elegant name with a dignified design. An arched entry gives special style to this home. Two window walls joining at a 90-degree angle and a two story high ceiling grace the great room. The right wing houses the master suite, a soothing place to go for private time. See photos ❶ 107, ❶ 122, ❷ 23.

BEDROOMS three + office

BATHROOMS 3 full + 2 halves

MASTER BEDROOM first floor

TOTAL AREA 4,024 sq. ft.

FIRST FLOOR 2,462 sq. ft.

OTHER FLOOR 1,562 sq. ft.

SIZE 75' x 59'

0 feet   10 feet   20 feet

³⁄₆₄ inch represents 1 foot

△ **Lindal**

© *Lindal Cedar Homes*

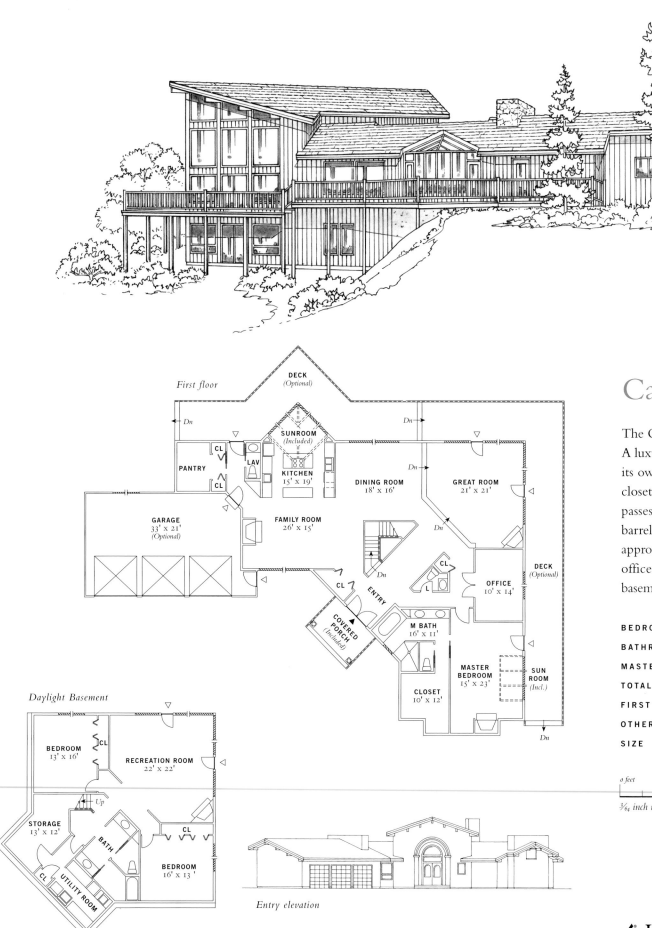

First floor

DECK
(Optional)

Dn

Dn

Dn

CL
PANTRY
LAV

CL

SUNROOM
(Included)

KITCHEN
15' x 19'

DINING ROOM
18' x 16'

GREAT ROOM
21' x 21'

GARAGE
33' x 21'
(Optional)

FAMILY ROOM
26' x 15'

Dn

CL

OFFICE
10' x 14'

DECK
(Optional)

ENTRY

Dn

CL

COVERED
PORCH
(Included)

M BATH
16' x 11'

MASTER
BEDROOM
15' x 23'

SUN
ROOM
(Incl.)

CLOSET
10' x 12'

Dn

Daylight Basement

BEDROOM
13' x 16'

CL

RECREATION ROOM
22' x 22'

Up

STORAGE
13' x 12'

BATH

CL

CL
UTILITY ROOM

BEDROOM
16' x 13'

Entry elevation

Casa Flora

The Casa Flora is a treasure of a home. A luxurious main floor master suite has its own fireplace, skywall, and walk-in closet. A hip-roofed sunroom encompasses an inviting breakfast nook. The barrel-vaulted entry creates a dramatic approach to the foyer. A main floor office, recreation area, and daylight basement complete this beauty.

BEDROOMS three + office

BATHROOMS 2 full + 2 half

MASTER BEDROOM first floor

TOTAL AREA 4,384 sq. ft.

FIRST FLOOR 2,845 sq. ft.

OTHER FLOOR 1,539 sq. ft.

SIZE 93' x 68'

0 feet   10 feet   20 feet

3/64 inch represents 1 foot

Lindal

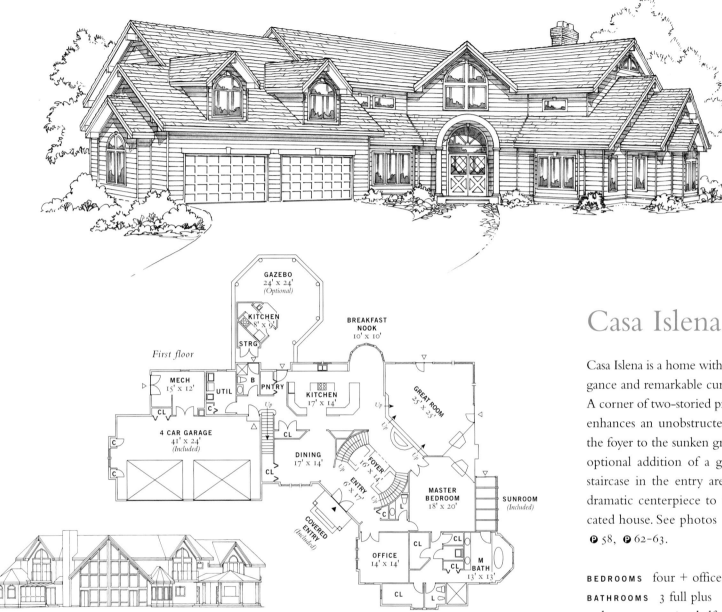

First floor

GAZEBO
24' x 24'
(Optional)

KITCHEN
8' x 9'

STRG

BREAKFAST
NOOK
10' x 10'

MECH
15' x 12'

UTIL

B

PNTRY

KITCHEN
17' x 14'

GREAT ROOM
25' x 25'

Up

CL

4 CAR GARAGE
41' x 24'
(Included)

C

C

CL

Up

DINING
17' x 14'

CL

FOYER
16' x 14'

Up

Up

Up

MASTER
BEDROOM
18' x 20'

SUNROOM
(Included)

ENTRY
6' x 17'

L

COVERED
ENTRY
(Included)

CL

C

OFFICE
14' x 14'

CL

CL

CL

M
BATH
13' x 13'

CL

L

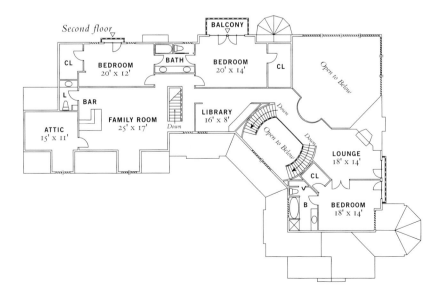

Rear elevation

Second floor

BALCONY

CL

BEDROOM
20' x 12'

BATH

BEDROOM
20' x 14'

CL

Open to Below

L

BAR

FAMILY ROOM
25' x 17'

Down

LIBRARY
16' x 8'

Down

Open to Below

ATTIC
15' x 11'

Open to Below

Down

LOUNGE
18' x 14'

CL

B

BEDROOM
18' x 14'

Casa Islena

Casa Islena is a home with spacious elegance and remarkable curbside appeal. A corner of two-storied prow windows enhances an unobstructed view from the foyer to the sunken great room. An optional addition of a grand custom staircase in the entry area provides a dramatic centerpiece to this sophisticated house. See photos ● 110, ℗ 26, ℗ 58, ℗ 62-63.

67

BEDROOMS four + office

BATHROOMS 3 full plus

1 three-quarter + 1 half

MASTER BEDROOM first floor

TOTAL AREA 6,742 sq. ft.

FIRST FLOOR 3,962 sq. ft.

OTHER FLOOR 2,780 sq. ft.

SIZE 116' x 74'

0 feet   10 feet   20 feet

1/27 inch represents 1 foot

△ **Lindal**

© Lindal Cedar Homes

CHALET
Vail

The chalet style Vail denotes a sense of coziness inside and out. Versatility is key in the floorplan of this home. Perfect as a first house, vacation home, or for people wanting to consolidate to a smaller living space. A balcony off the second floor master bedroom offers a great place to breathe in fresh morning air, while taking in the view.

BEDROOMS two

BATHROOMS 1 full + 1 half

MASTER BEDROOM second floor

TOTAL AREA 1,174 sq. ft.

FIRST FLOOR 608 sq. ft.

OTHER FLOOR 566 sq. ft.

SIZE 27' x 37'

First floor

LAV
DINING/FAMILY
15' x 10'
CL
KITCHEN
10' x 8'
Up
COVERED ENTRY
(Included)
LIVING ROOM
20' x 13'
DECK
(Optional)

Second floor

CL
BEDROOM
15' x 10'
B
Dn
CL
MASTER BEDROOM
20' x 11'
BALCONY

0 feet   10 feet   20 feet

¹⁄₁₆ inch represents 1 foot

Rear elevation

Lindal

© Lindal Cedar Homes

Aspen

The Aspen packs a lot of punch into minimal space. With the entry flowing to the kitchen, dining and great rooms, a surprising feeling of spaciousness is felt throughout this home. A loft on the second floor adds flexible space to put a game room, or home office.

BEDROOMS two

BATHROOMS 1 full

MASTER BEDROOM first floor

TOTAL AREA 1,189 sq. ft.

FIRST FLOOR 806 sq. ft.

OTHER FLOOR 383 sq. ft.

SIZE 27' x 30'

69

First floor

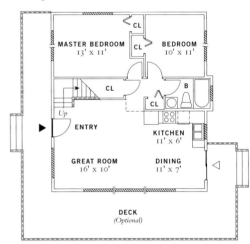

Second floor

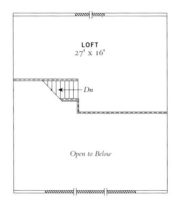

0 feet	10 feet	20 feet

1/16 inch represents 1 foot

Entry elevation

Lindal

© *Lindal Cedar Homes*

First floor

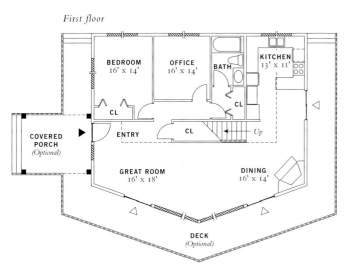

BEDROOM
16' x 14'

OFFICE
16' x 14'

BATH

KITCHEN
13' x 11'

CL

CL

CL

COVERED
PORCH
(Optional)

ENTRY

Up

GREAT ROOM
16' x 18'

DINING
16' x 14'

DECK
(Optional)

Second floor

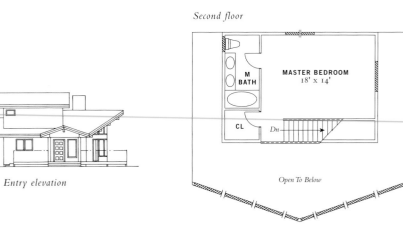

M
BATH

MASTER BEDROOM
18' x 14'

CL

Dn

Open To Below

Entry elevation

CONTEMPO PROW

Fraser

At home nestled into any environment, the Fraser with its compact footprint and spacious interior brings flexibility to its setting. This concise design offers main floor access to a bedroom and an office, an open dining and great room area, and an efficient kitchen layout. The second floor master suite becomes a personal abode where one can go to regroup.

BEDROOMS two + office

BATHROOMS 2 full

MASTER BEDROOM second floor

TOTAL AREA 1,508 sq. ft.

FIRST FLOOR 1,068 sq. ft.

OTHER FLOOR 440 sq. ft.

SIZE 37' x 32'

0 feet   10 feet   20 feet

1/16 inch represents 1 foot

Lindal

© Lindal Cedar Homes

First floor

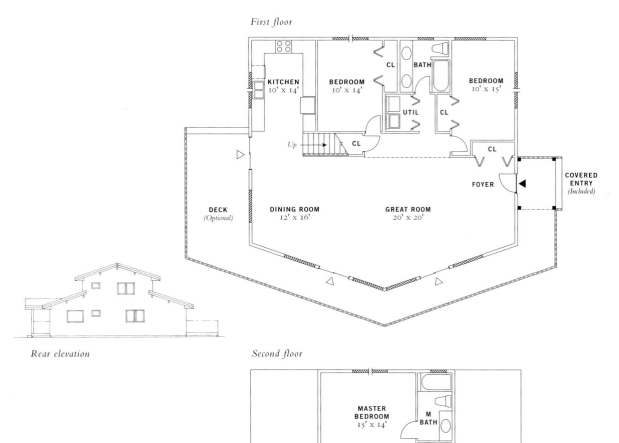

Rear elevation

Second floor

CONTEMPO PROW

St. Lawrence

St. Lawrence's layout is exceptionally well suited for any setting. An uninterrupted view from the entry to the great room creates a feeling of expanse. The master suite's location in the top-knot offers a private retreat. Spacious, open dining and great rooms create a multitude of possibilities for hosting an array of parties.

71

BEDROOMS three

BATHROOMS 2 full

MASTER BEDROOM second floor

TOTAL AREA 1,889 sq. ft.

FIRST FLOOR 1,517 sq. ft.

OTHER FLOOR 372 sq. ft.

SIZE 59' x 44'

0 feet   10 feet   20 feet

⅟₁₆ inch represents 1 foot

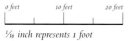

© Lindal Cedar Homes

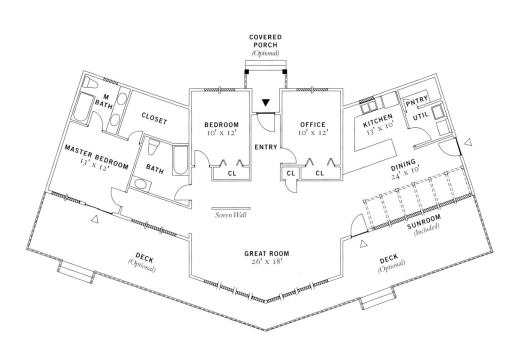

COVERED PORCH
(Optional)

M BATH

CLOSET

MASTER BEDROOM
13' x 12'

BATH

BEDROOM
10' x 12'

ENTRY

CL

OFFICE
10' x 12'

CL CL

KITCHEN
13' x 10'

PNTRY

UTIL

DINING
24' x 10'

Screen Wall

SUNROOM
(Included)

DECK
(Optional)

GREAT ROOM
26' x 18'

DECK
(Optional)

CapeSide

Drama and comfort come together in the CapeSide. When placed on a lot with abundant scenery, this home's nearly all glass view side and cathedral ceilings offer spectacular sights. The dining room flows into a large sunroom providing a one-of-a-kind eating area. An optional deck is a great addition for outside entertaining possibilities.

BEDROOMS two + office

BATHROOMS 2 full

MASTER BEDROOM first floor

TOTAL AREA 1,806 sq. ft.

FIRST FLOOR 1,806 sq. ft.

SIZE 75' x 37'

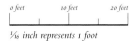

0 feet   10 feet   20 feet

1/16 inch represents 1 foot

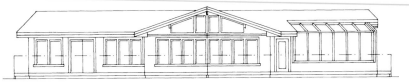

Rear elevation

Lindal

CONTEMPO PROW STAR

BaySide

Single floor living is enhanced with the BaySide's unique features. Its prow windows and main entry share the same side of the house, creating both great curbside appeal and scenic viewing. Three bedrooms, two full baths and a walk-in pantry in the kitchen finish this one floor wonder.

BEDROOMS three

BATHROOMS 2 full

MASTER BEDROOM first floor

TOTAL AREA 1,941 sq. ft.

FIRST FLOOR 1,941 sq. ft.

SIZE 66' x 36'

0 feet   10 feet   20 feet

⅟₁₆ inch represents 1 foot

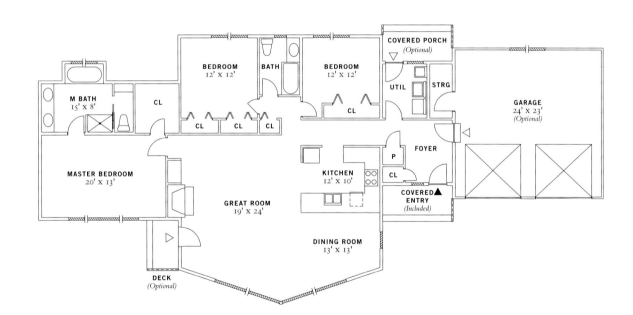

Rear elevation

Lindal

© *Lindal Cedar Homes*

First floor

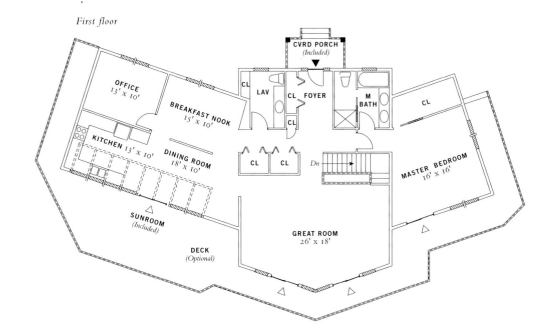

CVRD PORCH
(Included)

OFFICE
13' X 10'

BREAKFAST NOOK
15' X 10'

CL LAV CL FOYER M BATH CL

KITCHEN 13' X 10'

DINING ROOM
18' X 10'

CL

CL CL

Dn

MASTER BEDROOM
16' X 16'

SUNROOM
(Included)

DECK
(Optional)

GREAT ROOM
26' X 18'

Daylight Basement

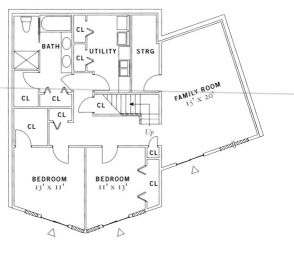

BATH

CL

UTILITY

STRG

CL CL

CL

CL

FAMILY ROOM
15' X 20'

CL

Up

BEDROOM
13' X 11'

BEDROOM
11' X 13'

CL

Entry elevation

CONTEMPO PROW STAR

CliffSide

The CliffSide's prow windows and expansive sunroom provide plenty of light-filled rooms to this home. An uninterrupted view from the entry to the great room creates open spaciousness. Added elements such as a cozy breakfast nook and convenient home office round out this versatile floorplan. See photos 🄛 12–13, 🄟 10.

BEDROOMS three + office

BATHROOMS 2 full + 1 half

MASTER BEDROOM first floor

TOTAL AREA 2,998 sq. ft.

FIRST FLOOR 1,790 sq. ft.

OTHER FLOOR 1,208 sq. ft.

SIZE 75' x 38'

0 feet	*10 feet*	*20 feet*

⅟₁₆ inch represents 1 foot

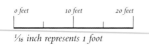

Lindal

© *Lindal Cedar Homes*

First floor

COVERED PORCH
(Included)

M BATH

CL

CL

CL

ENTRY

CL

MASTER BEDROOM
18' X 12'

LIVING
26' X 22'

LAV

CL

UTILITY

CL

PANTRY

KITCHEN

DINING

SUNROOM

Up

DECK
(Optional)

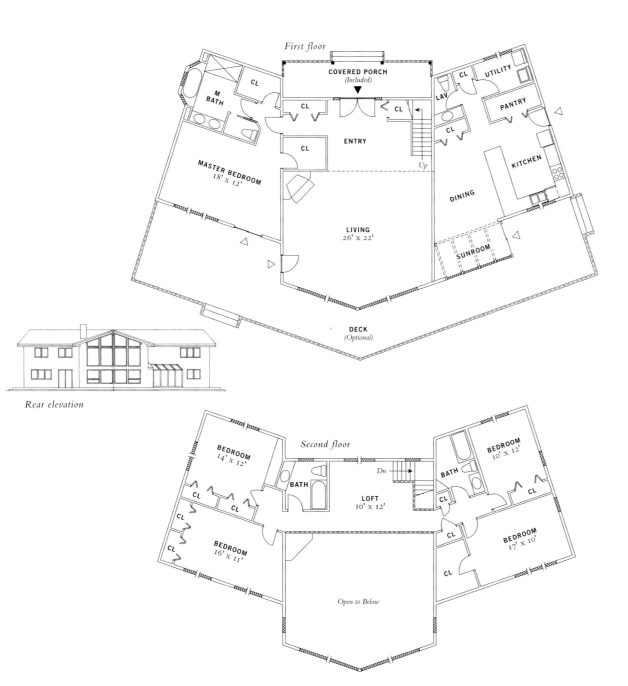

Rear elevation

Second floor

BEDROOM
14' X 12'

BATH

Dn

BATH

BEDROOM
10' X 12'

CL

CL

CL

LOFT
10' X 12'

CL

CL

CL

CL

BEDROOM
16' X 11'

CL

CL

BEDROOM
17' X 10'

Open to Below

CountrySide

The CountrySide is refreshingly crisp and clean in its design. The upper floor boasts amenities such as a spacious loft which can be used as a library or an office. Also available on the second floor is an unobstructed view from the balcony to the living area below. An optional corner fireplace and a walk-in pantry off the kitchen complete this best selling house.

BEDROOMS five

BATHROOMS 3 full + 1 half

MASTER BEDROOM first floor

TOTAL AREA 3,299 sq. ft.

FIRST FLOOR 1,948 sq. ft.

OTHER FLOOR 1,351 sq. ft.

SIZE 73' X 44'

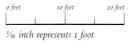

0 feet   10 feet   20 feet

¹⁄₁₆ inch represents 1 foot

75

Lindal

© *Lindal Cedar Homes*

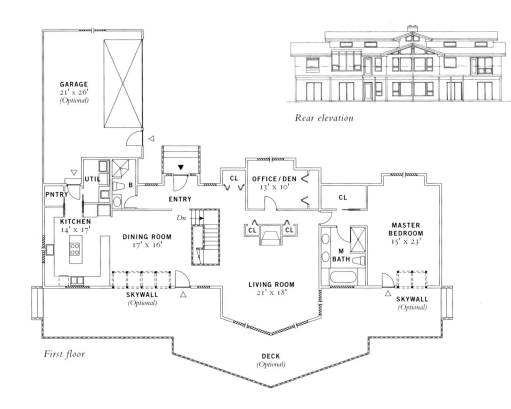

GARAGE
21' x 26'
(Optional)

UTIL

B

PNTRY

CL

OFFICE / DEN
13' x 10'

CL

MASTER
BEDROOM
15' x 23'

KITCHEN
14' x 17'

ENTRY

Dn

DINING ROOM
17' x 16'

CL

CL

M BATH

LIVING ROOM
21' x 18'

SKYWALL
(Optional)

SKYWALL
(Optional)

First floor

DECK
(Optional)

Rear elevation

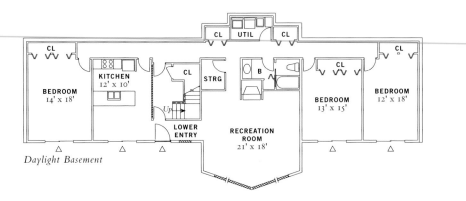

CL

UTIL

CL

CL

CL

BEDROOM
14' x 18'

KITCHEN
12' x 10'

CL

STRG

B

BEDROOM
13' x 15'

BEDROOM
12' x 18'

Up

LOWER
ENTRY

RECREATION
ROOM
21' x 18'

Daylight Basement

CONTEMPO PROW STAR

BrookSide

The BrookSide has a wealth of added touches. Two kitchens, one on each level, offer endless entertaining and living configurations. An optional skywall adds unobstructed viewing pleasure from the dining room. An office on the main floor is just one of the extras to this floorplan. Adding an optional clearstory, shown here, is a stylish way to let additional light into this home's interior. See photos ℗ 45.

BEDROOMS four + office

BATHROOMS 2 full + 1 three-quarter

MASTER BEDROOM first floor

TOTAL AREA 4,207 sq. ft.

FIRST FLOOR 2,153 sq. ft.

OTHER FLOOR 2,054 sq. ft.

SIZE 84' x 36'

0 feet   10 feet   20 feet

3/64 inch represents 1 foot

 Lindal

© Lindal Cedar Homes

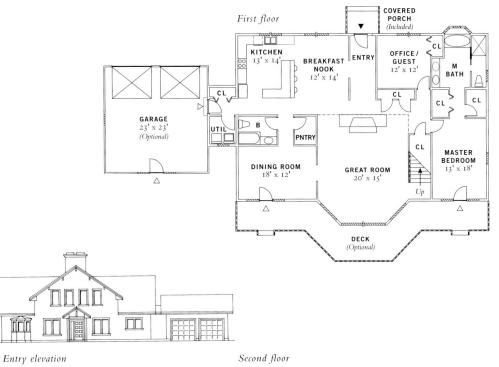

First floor

COVERED PORCH *(Included)*

KITCHEN 13' x 14'

BREAKFAST NOOK 12' x 14'

ENTRY

OFFICE/ GUEST 12' x 12'

CL

M BATH

CL

CL

CL

GARAGE 23' x 23' *(Optional)*

CL

UTIL

B

PNTRY

CL

MASTER BEDROOM 13' x 18'

DINING ROOM 18' x 12'

GREAT ROOM 20' x 15'

Up

DECK *(Optional)*

Entry elevation

Second floor

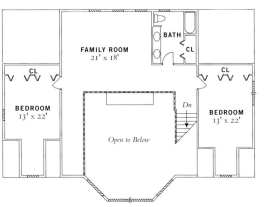

FAMILY ROOM 21' x 18'

BATH

CL

CL

CL

BEDROOM 13' x 22'

Dn

BEDROOM 13' x 22'

Open to Below

Meadowbrook

Meadowbrook's covered porch keeps elements at bay and gives shelter from inclement weather. Feelings of spaciousness begin outside and continue on throughout the interior. The main floor master bedroom provides privacy from the family room and two additional bedrooms located on the second floor. A breakfast nook off the kitchen becomes a place to pause and reflect before starting a hectic day. See photos ● 109, ● 113.

BEDROOMS three + office

BATHROOMS 3 full

MASTER BEDROOM first floor

TOTAL AREA 3,718 sq. ft.

FIRST FLOOR 2,342 sq. ft.

OTHER FLOOR 1,376 sq. ft.

SIZE 88' x 44'

0 feet   10 feet   20 feet

³⁄₆₄ inch represents 1 foot

◭ Lindal

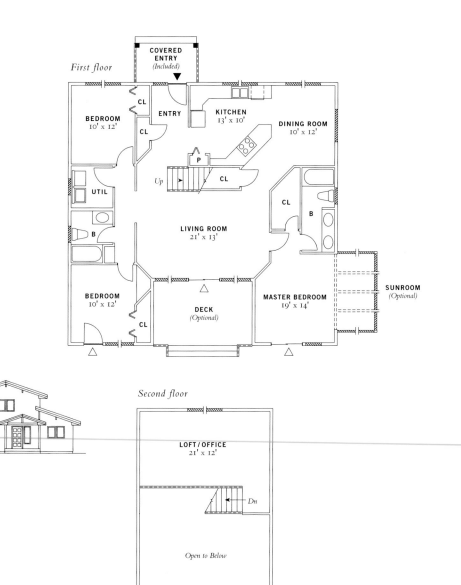

First floor

COVERED ENTRY *(Included)*

BEDROOM 10' x 12'

CL

CL

ENTRY

KITCHEN 13' x 10'

DINING ROOM 10' x 12'

UTIL

B

P

Up

CL

LIVING ROOM 21' x 13'

CL

B

BEDROOM 10' x 12'

CL

DECK *(Optional)*

MASTER BEDROOM 19' x 14'

SUNROOM *(Optional)*

Entry elevation

Second floor

LOFT/OFFICE 21' x 12'

Open to Below

Dn

PANORAMA

Monaco

Monaco's design encompasses practicality while embracing symmetry. This three bedroom u-shaped house includes a loft on the upper floor. The added space is flexible enough to bring virtually endless options to your home. A large deck enclosed on three sides provides hours of outside entertainment possibilities in a courtyard setting.

BEDROOMS three + office

BATHROOMS 2 full

MASTER BEDROOM first floor

TOTAL AREA 1,816 sq. ft.

FIRST FLOOR 1,537 sq. ft.

OTHER FLOOR 279 sq. ft.

SIZE 49' x 40'

0 feet   10 feet   20 feet

1/16 inch represents 1 foot

⏚ Lindal

Niagara

First floor

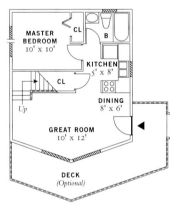

MASTER
BEDROOM
10' x 10'

CL

B

KITCHEN
5' x 8'

CL

Up

DINING
8' x 6'

GREAT ROOM
10' x 12'

DECK
(Optional)

Good things come in small packages. The Niagra's concise floorplan has an astonishingly spacious feeling to it. A double-storied prow gives a light, airy ambiance to the living and dining rooms. Upstairs a loft can be converted into storage space or a family room.

79

BEDROOMS one

BATHROOMS 1 full

MASTER BEDROOM first floor

TOTAL AREA 768 sq. ft.

FIRST FLOOR 507 sq. ft.

OTHER FLOOR 261 sq. ft.

SIZE 22' x 26'

0 feet   10 feet   20 feet

1/16 inch represents 1 foot

Entry elevation

Second floor

LOFT
27' x 16'

Dn

Open To Below

PROW

Coronado

First floor

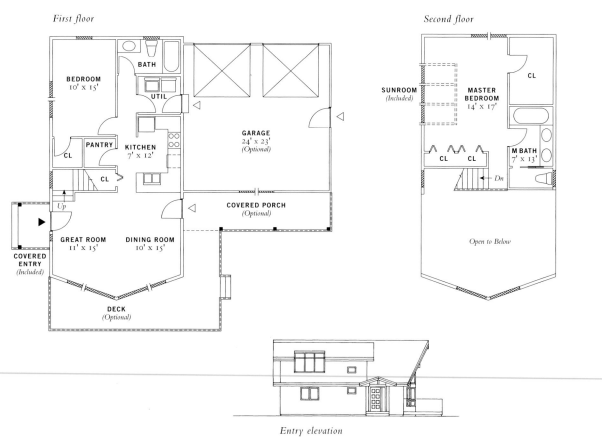

BEDROOM
10' x 15'

BATH

UTIL

PANTRY

KITCHEN
7' x 12'

CL

CL

GARAGE
24' x 23'
(Optional)

Up

COVERED PORCH
(Optional)

COVERED
ENTRY
(Included)

GREAT ROOM
11' x 15'

DINING ROOM
10' x 15'

DECK
(Optional)

Second floor

SUNROOM
(Included)

MASTER
BEDROOM
14' x 17'

CL

CL   CL

M BATH
7' x 13'

Dn

Open to Below

Entry elevation

The Coronado's covered porch greets visitors with a cozy cabin feeling. Measuring 36 feet without the optional garage, it's ideal for placement on a narrow lot. A walk-in pantry in the kitchen provides a great area to store extra supplies. The master suite's sunroom entices you to while away the hours in warm enjoyment.

BEDROOMS two

BATHROOMS 2 full

MASTER BEDROOM second floor

TOTAL AREA 1,294 sq. ft.

FIRST FLOOR 828 sq. ft.

OTHER FLOOR 466 sq. ft.

SIZE 76' x 36'

0 feet   10 feet   20 feet

⅟₁₆ inch represents 1 foot

△ Lindal

© *Lindal Cedar Homes*

Greenbriar

The appealing detail of Greenbriar's arched entryway sets it apart from other homes. A half round window, sidelights, and a formal covered porch provide distinctive design elements. The upper level becomes an area for privacy by encompassing the master suite and an adjoining loft, which can be used as an office or sitting room.

BEDROOMS three

BATHROOMS 2 full

MASTER BEDROOM second floor

TOTAL AREA 1,760 sq. ft.

FIRST FLOOR 1,153 sq. ft.

OTHER FLOOR 607 sq. ft.

SIZE 53' x 53'

```
0 feet        10 feet        20 feet
```
⅟₁₆ inch represents 1 foot

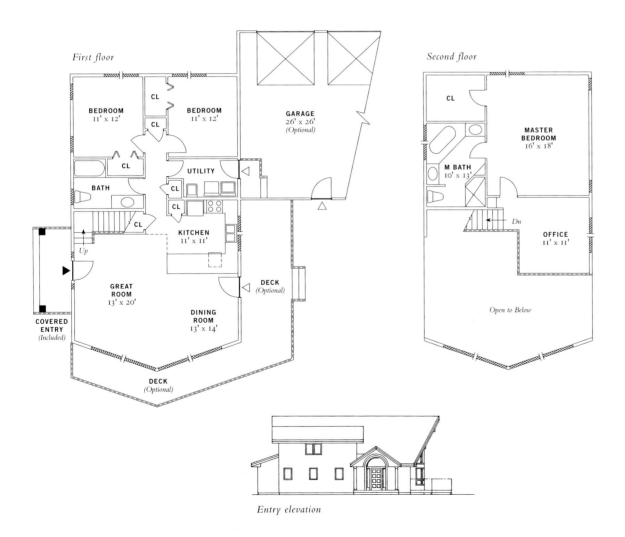

First floor

BEDROOM
11' x 12'

CL

BEDROOM
11' x 12'

CL

GARAGE
26' x 26'
(Optional)

CL

UTILITY

CL

BATH

CL

CL

KITCHEN
11' x 11'

CL

Up

GREAT
ROOM
13' x 20'

DECK
(Optional)

DINING
ROOM
13' x 14'

COVERED
ENTRY
(Included)

DECK
(Optional)

Second floor

CL

MASTER
BEDROOM
16' x 18'

M BATH
10' x 13'

Dn

OFFICE
11' x 11'

Open to Below

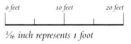

Entry elevation

▲ Lindal

© Lindal Cedar Homes

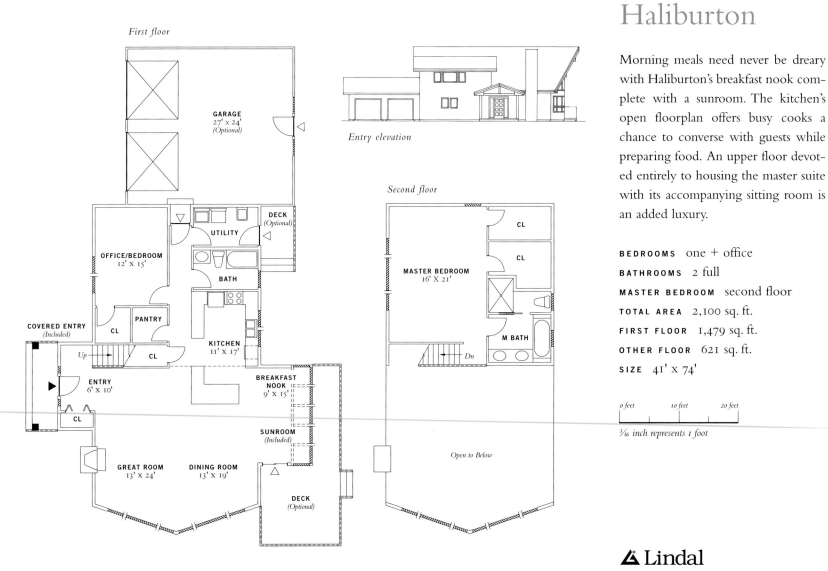

First floor

GARAGE
27' x 24'
(Optional)

DECK
(Optional)

UTILITY

OFFICE/BEDROOM
12' x 15'

BATH

COVERED ENTRY
(Included)

PANTRY

CL

CL

Up

CL

KITCHEN
11' x 17'

ENTRY
6' x 10'

BREAKFAST
NOOK
9' x 15'

CL

SUNROOM
(Included)

GREAT ROOM
13' x 24'

DINING ROOM
13' x 19'

DECK
(Optional)

Entry elevation

Second floor

CL

CL

MASTER BEDROOM
16' x 21'

M BATH

Dn

Open to Below

PROW

Haliburton

Morning meals need never be dreary with Haliburton's breakfast nook complete with a sunroom. The kitchen's open floorplan offers busy cooks a chance to converse with guests while preparing food. An upper floor devoted entirely to housing the master suite with its accompanying sitting room is an added luxury.

BEDROOMS one + office

BATHROOMS 2 full

MASTER BEDROOM second floor

TOTAL AREA 2,100 sq. ft.

FIRST FLOOR 1,479 sq. ft.

OTHER FLOOR 621 sq. ft.

SIZE 41' x 74'

0 feet   10 feet   20 feet

1/16 inch represents 1 foot

⛰ Lindal

© Lindal Cedar Homes

Capistrano

Just like its magical name, you'll want to return again and again to the Capistrano. A great design for a recreational home or a full time residence. The great room's windows create a wonderful opportunity to view nature's scenic canvas. An upstairs family room provides an area to join together and create warm memories.

BEDROOMS three

BATHROOMS 2 full + 1 half

MASTER BEDROOM first floor

TOTAL AREA 2,334 sq. ft.

FIRST FLOOR 1,493 sq. ft.

OTHER FLOOR 841 sq. ft.

SIZE 62' x 50'

83

First floor

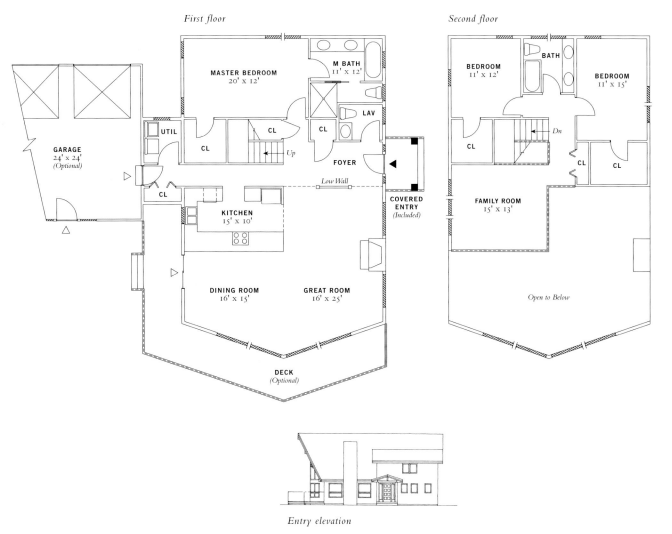

GARAGE
24' x 24'
(Optional)

MASTER BEDROOM
20' x 12'

M BATH
11' x 12'

LAV

UTIL

CL

CL

CL

CL

Up

FOYER

Low Wall

COVERED
ENTRY
(Included)

KITCHEN
15' x 10'

DINING ROOM
16' x 15'

GREAT ROOM
16' x 25'

DECK
(Optional)

Second floor

BEDROOM
11' x 12'

BATH

BEDROOM
11' x 15'

CL

Dn

CL

CL

FAMILY ROOM
15' x 13'

Open to Below

0 feet   10 feet   20 feet

1/16 inch represents 1 foot

Entry elevation

© Lindal Cedar Homes

First floor

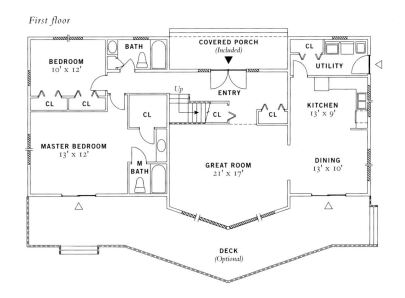

BATH

BEDROOM
10' x 12'

CL

UTILITY

COVERED PORCH
(Included)

ENTRY

Up

CL

CL

CL

KITCHEN
13' x 9'

CL

MASTER BEDROOM
13' x 12'

M
BATH

GREAT ROOM
21' x 17'

DINING
13' x 10'

DECK
(Optional)

Entry elevation

Second floor

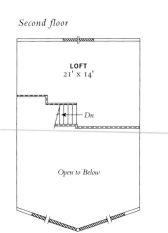

LOFT
21' x 14'

Dn

Open to Below

PROW STAR

CascadeVista

CascadeVista's floorplan creates end-less opportunities to personalize your home. A well-sized kitchen has space to add an island with an eating bar. The loft located on the upper floor is the perfect spot for a library, family room, den, or cozy sitting room.

BEDROOMS two

BATHROOMS 2 full

MASTER BEDROOM first floor

TOTAL AREA 1,821 sq. ft.

FIRST FLOOR 1,551 sq. ft.

OTHER FLOOR 270 sq. ft.

SIZE 59' x 32'

0 feet   10 feet   20 feet

1/16 inch represents 1 foot

 Lindal

© *Lindal Cedar Homes*

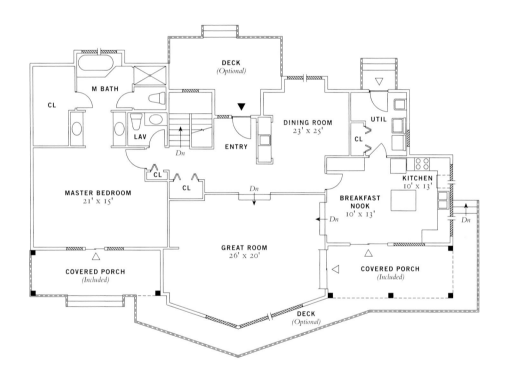

DECK
(Optional)

M BATH

CL

LAV

DINING ROOM
23' x 25'

UTIL

CL

ENTRY

Dn

CL

CL

MASTER BEDROOM
21' x 15'

CL

KITCHEN
10' x 13'

Dn

BREAKFAST
NOOK
10' x 13'

Dn

GREAT ROOM
26' x 20'

Dn

COVERED PORCH
(Included)

COVERED PORCH
(Included)

DECK
(Optional)

Entry elevation

ViewVista

The slightly different configuration of the ViewVista's prow windows create a relaxing atmosphere in which to capture incredible views. The master suite with its own covered porch has a private sanctuary feeling. The layout includes a kitchen that is open to the great room creating a sense of togetherness during meal preparation.

BEDROOMS one

BATHROOMS 1 full + 1 half

MASTER BEDROOM first floor

TOTAL AREA 1,920 sq. ft.

FIRST FLOOR 1,920 sq. ft.

SIZE 67' x 43'

0 feet   10 feet   20 feet

1/16 inch represents 1 foot

⚜ Lindal

© Lindal Cedar Homes

First floor

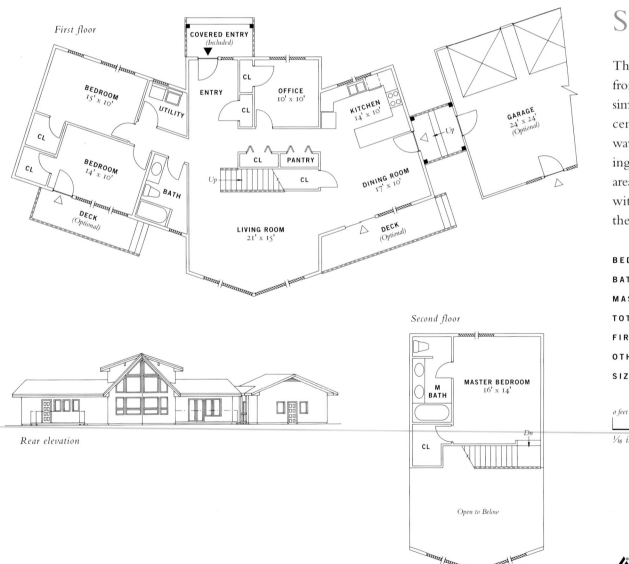

COVERED ENTRY
(Included)

BEDROOM
15' x 10'

CL

CL

ENTRY

CL

CL

OFFICE
10' x 10'

UTILITY

KITCHEN
14' x 10'

BEDROOM
14' x 10'

BATH

CL   PANTRY

Up

CL

DINING ROOM
17' x 10'

Up

GARAGE
24' x 24'
(Optional)

DECK
(Optional)

LIVING ROOM
21' x 15'

DECK
(Optional)

Rear elevation

Second floor

MASTER BEDROOM
16' x 14'

M
BATH

Dn

CL

Open to Below

SeaVista

The beauty of the SeaVista comes from its articulated covered entry and simple design elements. An office adjacent to the foyer offers a convenient way to receive clients without traveling through the home's more private areas. Add an optional garage complete with breezeway that leads directly to the kitchen and dining room.

BEDROOMS three + office

BATHROOMS 2 full

MASTER BEDROOM second floor

TOTAL AREA 1,992 sq. ft.

FIRST FLOOR 1,613 sq. ft.

OTHER FLOOR 379 sq. ft.

SIZE 98' x 45'

0 feet   10 feet   20 feet

1⁄16 inch represents 1 foot

Lindal

© *Lindal Cedar Homes*

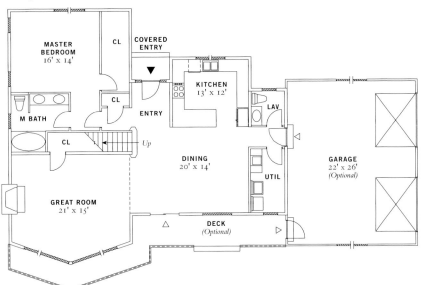

First floor

MASTER BEDROOM
16' x 14'

CL

COVERED ENTRY

CL

M BATH

KITCHEN
13' x 12'

LAV

CL

ENTRY

Up

DINING
20' x 14'

UTIL

GARAGE
22' x 26'
(Optional)

GREAT ROOM
21' x 15'

DECK
(Optional)

Second floor

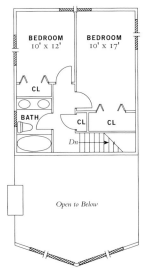

BEDROOM
10' x 12'

BEDROOM
10' x 17'

CL

BATH

CL

CL

Dn

Open to Below

Entry elevation

SkyVista

The SkyVista's two-story prow windows offer spectacular views of the sky and beyond. The covered entry tucked neatly into a sheltered corner provides an area to get away from less than favorable weather. An addition of an optional fireplace in the great room creates a warm centerpiece to this home.

BEDROOMS three

BATHROOMS 2 full + 1 half

MASTER BEDROOM first floor

TOTAL AREA 2,023 sq. ft.

FIRST FLOOR 1,543 sq. ft.

OTHER FLOOR 480 sq. ft.

SIZE 48' x 43'

0 feet   10 feet   20 feet

⅟₁₆ inch represents 1 foot

87

Lindal

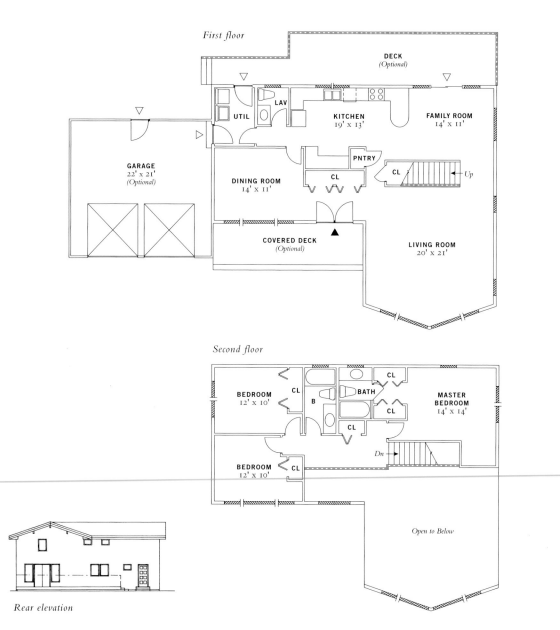

First floor

DECK
(Optional)

UTIL LAV

KITCHEN
19' x 13'

FAMILY ROOM
14' x 11'

GARAGE
22' x 21'
(Optional)

DINING ROOM
14' x 11'

PNTRY

CL

CL

Up

COVERED DECK
(Optional)

LIVING ROOM
20' x 21'

Second floor

BEDROOM
12' x 10'

CL

B

CL

BATH

CL

CL

MASTER
BEDROOM
14' x 14'

Dn

BEDROOM
12' x 10'

CL

Open to Below

Rear elevation

PROW STAR

Woodlawn

Many attractive aspects are incorporated into this family oriented home. The Woodlawn's bedrooms are located on the upper level with the common areas positioned on the main floor, creating two distinctive living spaces. This house also has ample closet and storage space. With a family and living room, there are plenty of options for gatherings.

BEDROOMS three

BATHROOMS 2 full + 1 half

MASTER BEDROOM second floor

TOTAL AREA 2,032 sq. ft.

FIRST FLOOR 1,279 sq. ft.

OTHER FLOOR 753 sq. ft.

SIZE 46' x 38'

0 feet   10 feet   20 feet

⅟₁₆ inch represents 1 foot

⚠ Lindal

© *Lindal Cedar Homes*

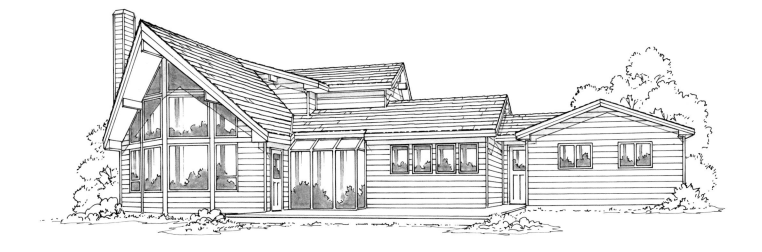

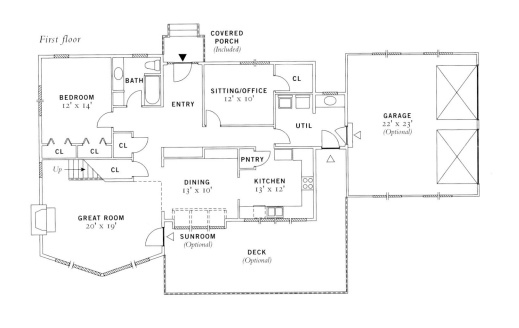

First floor

COVERED PORCH *(Included)*

BATH

BEDROOM 12' x 14'

ENTRY

SITTING/OFFICE 12' x 10'

CL

UTIL

GARAGE 22' x 23' *(Optional)*

CL

CL   CL

CL

Up

CL

PNTRY

DINING 13' x 10'

KITCHEN 13' x 12'

GREAT ROOM 20' x 19'

SUNROOM *(Optional)*

DECK *(Optional)*

PROW STAR
LakeVista

The outer radiance of the LakeVista is enhanced by its efficient inner design. The master suite is tucked into the upper floor providing an intimate get-away. An office space located on the main floor creates an organized place to work or can double as a third bedroom. A large kitchen with plenty of space to prepare meals is an added plus.

BEDROOMS two + office
BATHROOMS 2 full
MASTER BEDROOM second floor
TOTAL AREA 2,101 sq. ft.
FIRST FLOOR 1,498 sq. ft.
OTHER FLOOR 603 sq. ft.
SIZE 76' x 37'

0 feet   10 feet   20 feet

1/16 inch represents 1 foot

BALCONY

Second floor

BATH 13' x 8'

MASTER BEDROOM 20' x 14'

CLOSET 13' x 7'

CL   CL

Dn

Open to Below

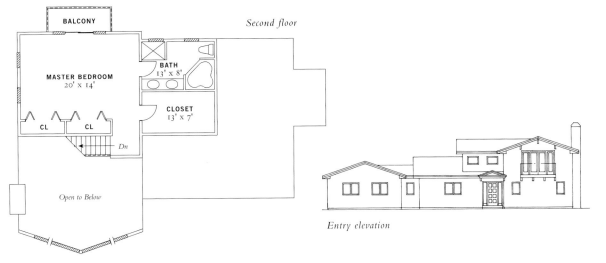

Entry elevation

Lindal

© *Lindal Cedar Homes*

First floor

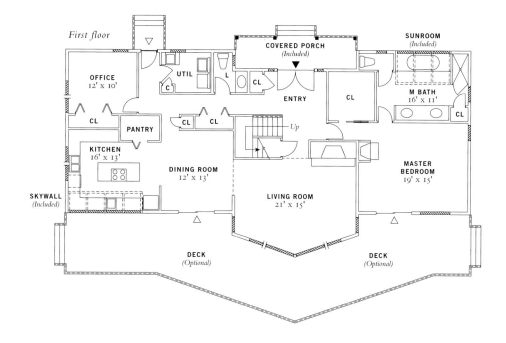

COVERED PORCH
(Included)

SUNROOM
(Included)

OFFICE
12' x 10'

UTIL

L

CL

ENTRY

CL

M BATH
16' x 11'

CL

CL

PANTRY

CL

CL

Up

KITCHEN
16' x 13'

DINING ROOM
12' x 13'

MASTER
BEDROOM
19' x 15'

SKYWALL
(Included)

LIVING ROOM
21' x 15'

DECK
(Optional)

DECK
(Optional)

Rear elevation

Second floor

BEDROOM
16' x 13'

B

Dn

CL

Open to Below

PROW STAR

ShoreVista

Open ShoreVista's double-door entry and an unobstructed view awaits you through the living room's two-storied prow windows. Create a rejuvenating hideaway by adding an optional sunroom and soaking tub to the master bathroom. A nicely sized office fits into a main floor corner and has its own convenient outer entry.

BEDROOMS two + office

BATHROOMS 2 full + 1 half

MASTER BEDROOM first floor

TOTAL AREA 2,266 sq. ft.

FIRST FLOOR 1,874 sq. ft.

OTHER FLOOR 392 sq. ft.

SIZE 68' x 34'

0 feet   10 feet   20 feet

¹⁄₆₄ inch represents 1 foot

⧉ Lindal

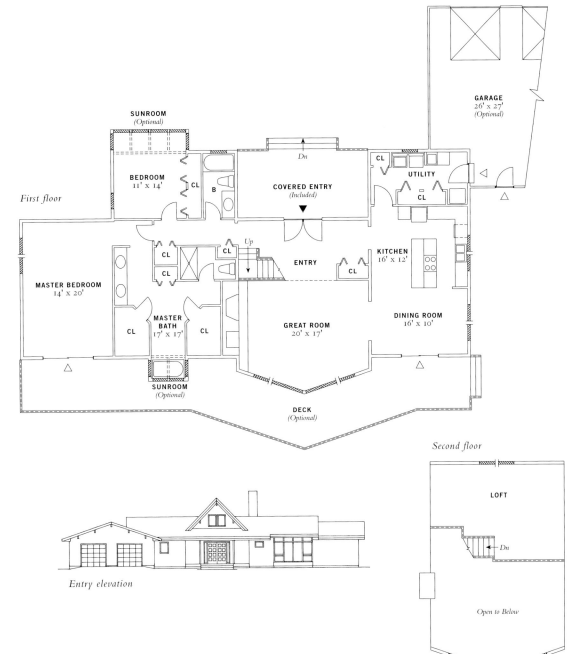

SUNROOM
(Optional)

First floor

BEDROOM
11' x 14'

MASTER BEDROOM
14' x 20'

MASTER
BATH
17' x 17'

CL

CL

CL

CL

CL

B

Dn

COVERED ENTRY
(Included)

Up

ENTRY

UTILITY

CL

CL

CL

KITCHEN
16' x 12'

GREAT ROOM
20' x 17'

DINING ROOM
16' x 10'

SUNROOM
(Optional)

DECK
(Optional)

GARAGE
26' x 27'
(Optional)

Entry elevation

Second floor

LOFT

Dn

Open to Below

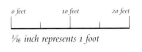

PROW STAR

MountainVista

The MountainVista boasts well-sized areas for nearly every room with plenty of space to create your own hideaway in the master suite. It contains two walk-in closets, a generous master bath, and a place for linen storage. Add a fireplace in the great room and it's a warm place to star gaze out the prow windows.

BEDROOMS two

BATHROOMS 2 full

MASTER BEDROOM first floor

TOTAL AREA 2,276 sq. ft.

FIRST FLOOR 1,992 sq. ft.

OTHER FLOOR 284 sq. ft.

SIZE 71' X 41'

0 feet   10 feet   20 feet

1/16 inch represents 1 foot

91

© Lindal Cedar Homes

SUMMIT

Whitney

First floor

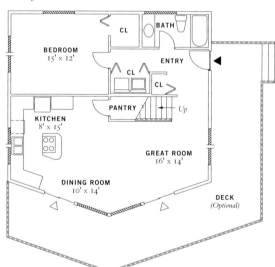

BEDROOM
15' x 12'

CL

BATH

ENTRY

CL

CL

PANTRY · Up

KITCHEN
8' x 15'

GREAT ROOM
16' x 14'

DINING ROOM
10' x 14'

DECK
(Optional)

Second floor

MASTER BEDROOM
15' x 12'

CL

M
BATH

Dn

Open to Below

A perfect home in which to ease into a relaxing evening, the Whitney has many nice features in a smaller plan. The main floor's spaciousness is felt throughout the open kitchen, dining, and great rooms. The upper floor boasts a well-sized master suite removed from common areas.

BEDROOMS two

BATHROOMS 2 full

MASTER BEDROOM second floor

TOTAL AREA 1,223 sq. ft.

FIRST FLOOR 917 sq. ft.

OTHER FLOOR 306 sq. ft.

SIZE 32' x 31'

0 feet   10 feet   20 feet

1/16 inch represents 1 foot

Entry elevation

▲ Lindal

© *Lindal Cedar Homes*

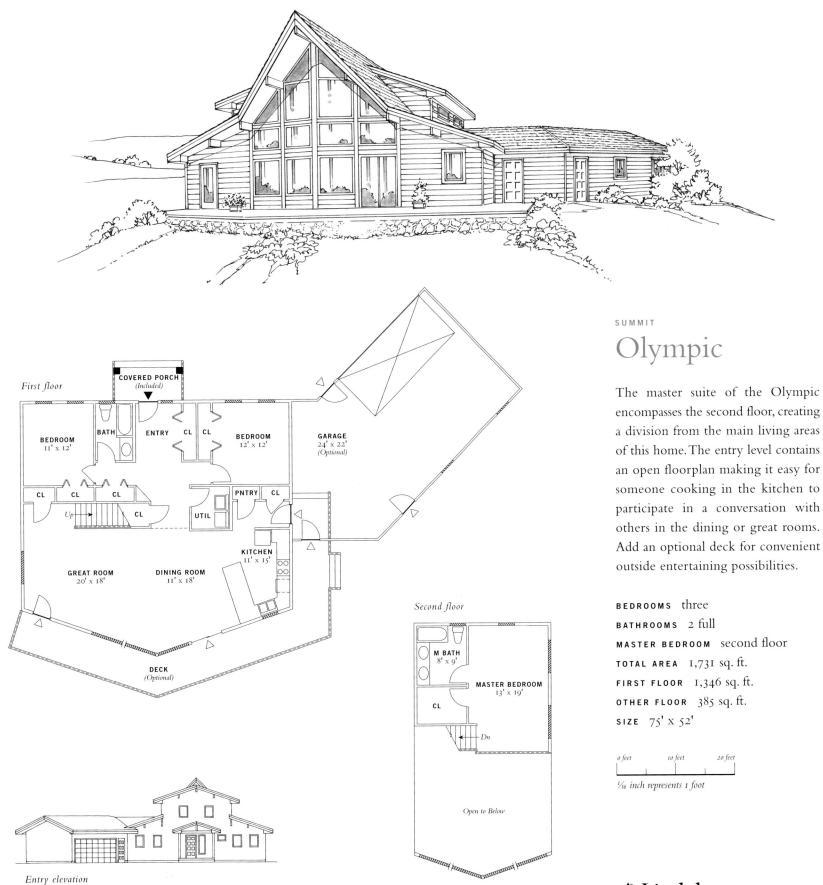

First floor

COVERED PORCH
(Included)

BEDROOM
11' x 12'

BATH

ENTRY

CL CL

BEDROOM
12' x 12'

GARAGE
24' x 22'
(Optional)

CL CL CL

CL

Up

PNTRY CL

UTIL

KITCHEN
11' x 15'

GREAT ROOM
20' x 18'

DINING ROOM
11' x 18'

DECK
(Optional)

Second floor

M BATH
8' x 9'

MASTER BEDROOM
13' x 19'

CL

Dn

Open to Below

Entry elevation

SUMMIT
Olympic

The master suite of the Olympic encompasses the second floor, creating a division from the main living areas of this home. The entry level contains an open floorplan making it easy for someone cooking in the kitchen to participate in a conversation with others in the dining or great rooms. Add an optional deck for convenient outside entertaining possibilities.

BEDROOMS three

BATHROOMS 2 full

MASTER BEDROOM second floor

TOTAL AREA 1,731 sq. ft.

FIRST FLOOR 1,346 sq. ft.

OTHER FLOOR 385 sq. ft.

SIZE 75' x 52'

0 feet   10 feet   20 feet

1/16 inch represents 1 foot

Lindal

© Lindal Cedar Homes

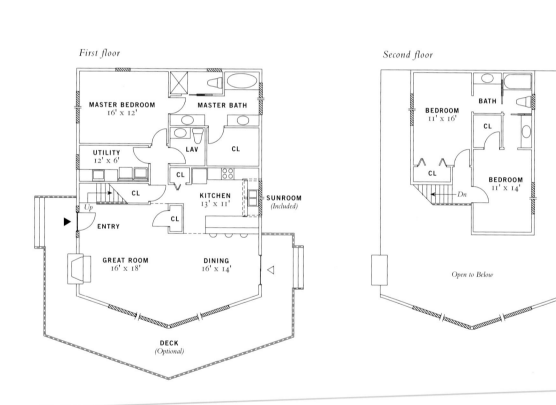

First floor

MASTER BEDROOM
16' x 12'

MASTER BATH

UTILITY
12' x 6'

LAV

CL

CL

CL

CL

KITCHEN
13' x 11'

SUNROOM
(Included)

CL

Up

ENTRY

GREAT ROOM
16' x 18'

DINING
16' x 14'

DECK
(Optional)

Second floor

BEDROOM
11' x 16'

BATH

CL

CL

CL

Dn

BEDROOM
11' x 14'

Open to Below

SUMMIT

Teton

The Teton's classic design offers the best of both worlds. The prow adds a sense of drama while the change in roof pitch creates a warm, rustic feeling, making a great place to relax and enjoy the view. A main floor master suite has plenty of space to kick off your shoes and rest. A skywall in the kitchen provides cooking with a view.

BEDROOMS three
BATHROOMS 2 full + 1 half
MASTER BEDROOM first floor
TOTAL AREA 1,741 sq. ft.
FIRST FLOOR 1,157 sq. ft.
OTHER FLOOR 584 sq. ft.
SIZE 32' x 44'

0 feet   10 feet   20 feet

1/16 inch represents 1 foot

Entry elevation

 Lindal

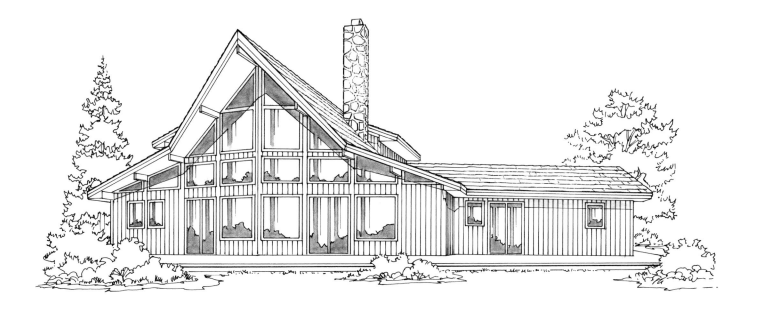

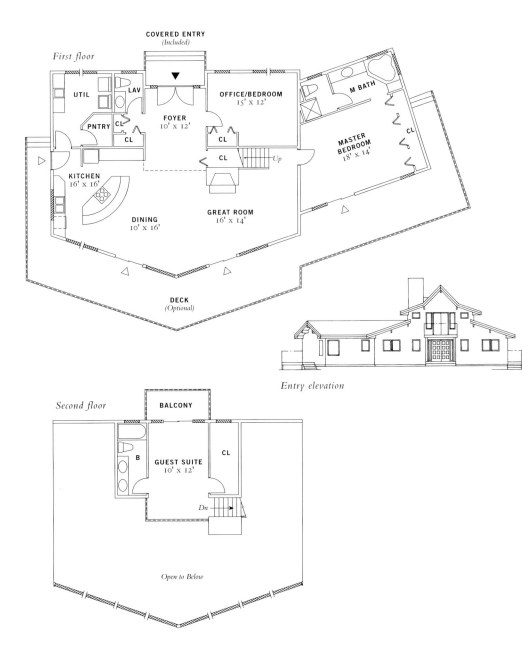

First floor

COVERED ENTRY
(Included)

UTIL

LAV

OFFICE/BEDROOM
15' x 12'

M BATH

FOYER
10' x 12'

PNTRY

CL

CL

CL

CL

CL

MASTER
BEDROOM
18' x 14'

Up

KITCHEN
16' x 16'

GREAT ROOM
16' x 14'

DINING
10' x 16'

DECK
(Optional)

Entry elevation

Second floor

BALCONY

B

GUEST SUITE
10' x 12'

CL

Dn

Open to Below

Newport

Boundless design is the key to the Newport's attractiveness. An open entry, kitchen, dining, and great room provide a sense of freedom and release. The office on the main floor creates a tranquil area in which to work and think. The extra bedroom located on the upper floor has its own balcony to view the great outdoors.

BEDROOMS two + office

BATHROOMS 2 full + 1 half

MASTER BEDROOM first floor

TOTAL AREA 2,064 sq. ft.

FIRST FLOOR 1,740 sq. ft.

OTHER FLOOR 324 sq. ft.

SIZE 65' x 38'

0 feet   *10 feet*   *20 feet*

⅟₁₆ inch represents 1 foot

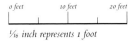

Lindal

Contemporary

Contemporary Lindal homes are the height of modern originality. Their eclectic good looks draw from a wealth of complementary influences to create a fresh expression of residential style. Outside, clean, uncluttered lines make a strong architectural statement that shows respect for the natural environment. Inside, a boundless flow of spaces provides unparalleled freedom to create your own person-alized living areas. Form follows function in the most intelligent, inspiring way. Some owners say that living in a Contemporary Lindal is like living in an uplifting work of art — with all the comforts of home.

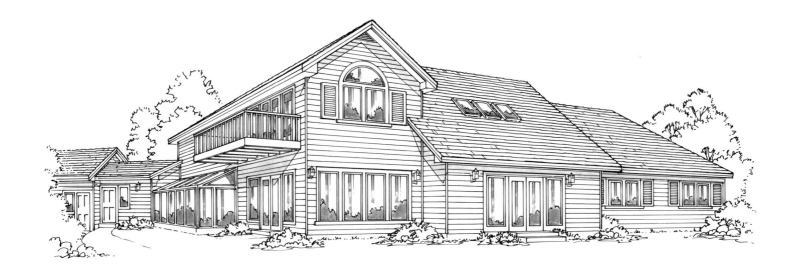

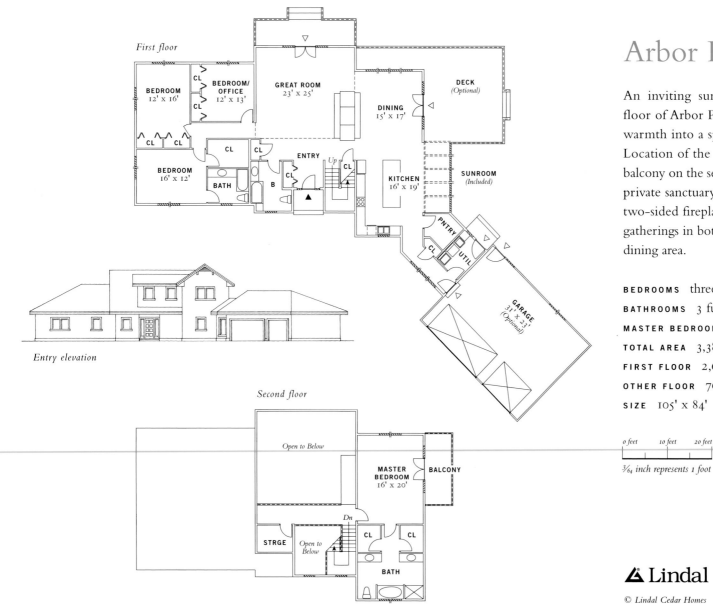

First floor

BEDROOM 12' x 16'	CL	BEDROOM/OFFICE 12' x 13'	GREAT ROOM 23' x 25'

CL

CL   CL

DECK (Optional)

DINING 15' x 17'

BEDROOM 16' x 12'

CL   CL

BATH   B

ENTRY   Up   CL

KITCHEN 16' x 19'

SUNROOM (Included)

PNTRY   UTIL   CL

GARAGE 31' x 23' (Optional)

Entry elevation

Second floor

Open to Below

MASTER BEDROOM 16' x 20'   BALCONY

Dn

STRGE   Open to Below   CL   CL

BATH

Arbor Place

An inviting sunroom on the main floor of Arbor Place floods light and warmth into a spacious kitchen area. Location of the master bedroom and balcony on the second floor provides a private sanctuary. Roaring fires in the two-sided fireplace will provide cozy gatherings in both the great room and dining area.

BEDROOMS three + office

BATHROOMS 3 full

MASTER BEDROOM second floor

TOTAL AREA 3,387 sq. ft.

FIRST FLOOR 2,625 sq. ft.

OTHER FLOOR 762 sq. ft.

SIZE 105' x 84'

0 feet   10 feet   20 feet

³⁄₆₄ inch represents 1 foot

Lindal

© *Lindal Cedar Homes*

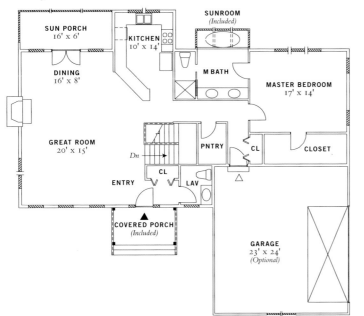

First floor

SUN PORCH
16' x 6'

SUNROOM
(Included)

KITCHEN
10' x 14'

DINING
16' x 8'

M BATH

MASTER BEDROOM
17' x 14'

GREAT ROOM
20' x 15'

Dn

PNTRY

CL

CLOSET

CL

ENTRY

LAV

COVERED PORCH
(Included)

GARAGE
23' x 24'
(Optional)

Daylight Basement

BEDROOM
13' x 13'

FAMILY ROOM
/OFFICE
12' x 12'

CL

CL

UTIL

Up

BEDROOM
13' x 13'

CL

CL

BATH

Rear elevation

Caribou Ridge

Caribou Ridge is a comfortable home that welcomes you in with its covered porch. Inside, sensible design elements create plenty of closet and storage space. A sunroom off the master bath offers an area for restful retreat. The covered porch off the dining room provides an inviting space for outdoor meals. An upstairs office area can double as a family room.

BEDROOMS   three + office

BATHROOMS   2 full + 1 half

MASTER BEDROOM   first floor

TOTAL AREA   2,294 sq. ft.

FIRST FLOOR   1,362 sq. ft.

OTHER FLOOR   932 sq. ft.

SIZE   57' x 51'

0 feet   *10 feet*   *20 feet*

1/16 *inch represents 1 foot*

△ **Lindal**

© *Lindal Cedar Homes*

First floor

DECK
(Optional)

Dn   Dn

Dn

LIVING ROOM
15' x 21'

Dn

DINING ROOM
16' x 11'

BEDROOM
11' x 15'

CL

KITCHEN
11' x 11'

BATH

Dn

CL

CL

UTIL

Up

FOYER

CL

GARAGE
21' x 21'
(Optional)

**COVERED
ENTRY**
(Included)

**SUNROOM/
BREAKFAST**
11' x 10'
(Included)

Second floor

SKYWALL
(Included)

BALCONY

Open to Below

BEDROOM
11' x 15'

MASTER BEDROOM
16' x 14'

CL

BATH

SITTING ROOM
12' x 11'

CL

BEDROOM
14' x 10'

Dn

CL

*Open to
Below*

CL

**M
BATH**

Westchester

The Westchester's design offers plenty of light-filled rooms. A sunroom off the breakfast nook provides a relaxing ambiance to start the day off right. The second floor's skywall can be viewed from the sitting room that accompanies the master suite. Add an optional fireplace in the living room and increase the natural warmth felt throughout this home.

BEDROOMS four
BATHROOMS 3 full
MASTER BEDROOM second floor
TOTAL AREA 2,443 sq. ft.
FIRST FLOOR 1,447 sq. ft.
OTHER FLOOR 996 sq. ft.
SIZE 43' x 64'

0 feet   *10 feet*   *20 feet*

1/16 inch represents 1 foot

Entry elevation

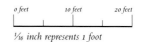

© Lindal Cedar Homes

Conway

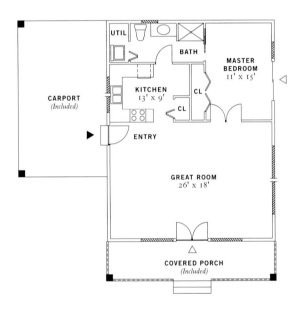

The compact floorplan of the Conway makes it an ideal choice for a cozy cabin getaway. Its covered porch entry leads to an expansive great room. A carport off the side of the house provides shelter for vehicles. This home's conveniently concise design makes use of every inch of its space.

BEDROOMS one

BATHROOMS 1 three quarter

MASTER BEDROOM first floor

TOTAL AREA 907 sq. ft.

FIRST FLOOR 907 sq. ft.

SIZE 27' x 34'

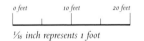

⅟₁₆ inch represents 1 foot

Entry elevation

Lindal

© Lindal Cedar Homes

First floor

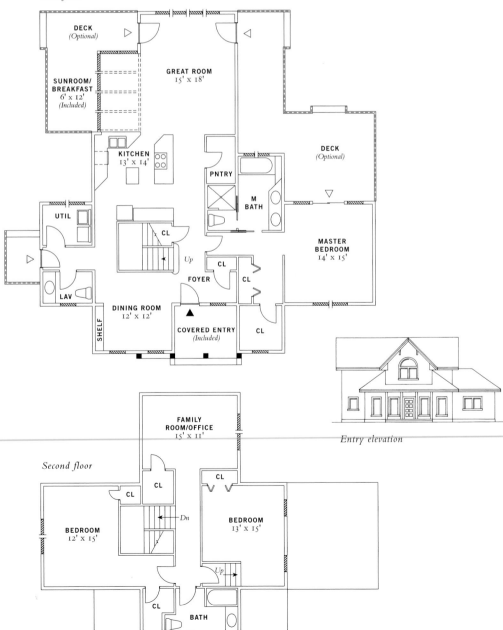

DECK
(Optional)

SUNROOM/
BREAKFAST
6' x 12'
(Included)

GREAT ROOM
15' x 18'

KITCHEN
13' x 14'

PNTRY

DECK
(Optional)

UTIL

CL

M
BATH

LAV

CL
FOYER
CL

MASTER
BEDROOM
14' x 15'

SHELF

DINING ROOM
12' x 12'

COVERED ENTRY
(Included)

CL

Second floor

FAMILY
ROOM/OFFICE
15' x 11'

CL

CL

CL

Dn

BEDROOM
12' x 15'

BEDROOM
13' x 15'

Up

CL

BATH

Entry elevation

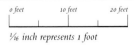

Corvallis

The Corvallis is a comfortable two level home with many niceties. A covered entry lends itself to old-fashioned charm with a modern flair. The sunroom/breakfast nook entices you to dine in a casual but inviting fashion. An addition of an optional deck off the great room provides an excellent area to hold summer barbeques with neighbors and friends.

BEDROOMS three + office
BATHROOMS 2 full + 1 half
MASTER BEDROOM first floor
TOTAL AREA 2,600 sq. ft.
FIRST FLOOR 1,690 sq. ft.
OTHER FLOOR 910 sq. ft.
SIZE 53' x 54'

0 feet   10 feet   20 feet

⅟₁₆ inch represents 1 foot

⌂ Lindal

© Lindal Cedar Homes

First floor

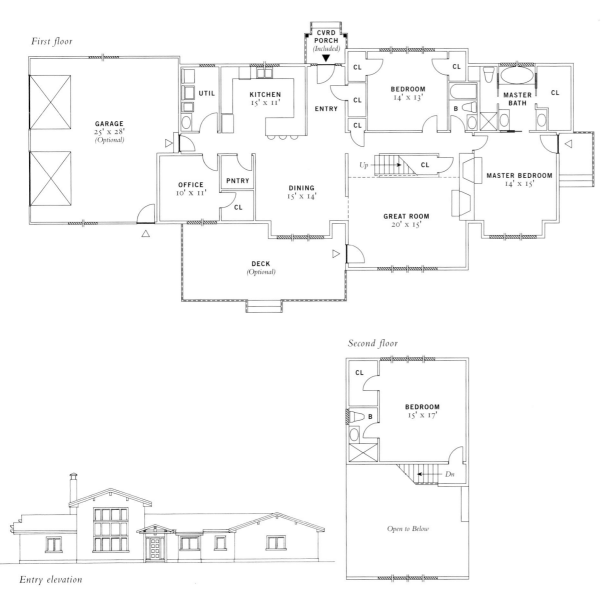

CVRD PORCH *(Included)*

GARAGE 25' x 28' *(Optional)*

UTIL

KITCHEN 15' x 11'

ENTRY

CL

CL

CL

BEDROOM 14' x 13'

CL

B

MASTER BATH

CL

OFFICE 10' x 11'

PNTRY

CL

DINING 15' x 14'

Up

CL

MASTER BEDROOM 14' x 15'

GREAT ROOM 20' x 15'

DECK *(Optional)*

Second floor

CL

B

BEDROOM 15' x 17'

Dn

Open to Below

Entry elevation

Craftsman

Long, clean lines, exposed rafters, and a covered porch entry grace the timeless design of the Craftsman. Curl up with a good book in an optional cozy window seat, located in the dining room or the master bedroom. An office area provides a great place to think and get away from it all. Reference ● 45 for a similar plan.

103

BEDROOMS three + office

BATHROOMS 2 full + 1 three quarter

MASTER BEDROOM first floor

TOTAL AREA 2,493 sq. ft.

FIRST FLOOR 2,093 sq. ft.

OTHER FLOOR 400 sq. ft.

SIZE 94' x 37'

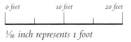

0 feet   10 feet   20 feet

1/16 inch represents 1 foot

△ Lindal

© Lindal Cedar Homes

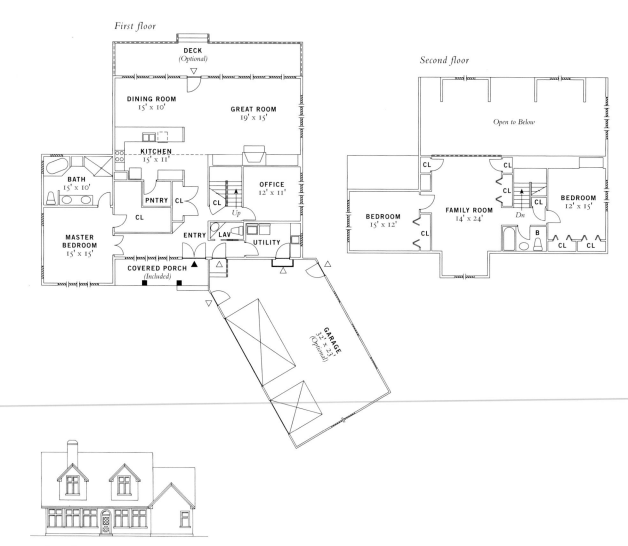

First floor

DECK
(Optional)

DINING ROOM
15' x 10'

GREAT ROOM
19' x 15'

KITCHEN
15' x 11'

BATH
15' x 10'

PNTRY   CL

CL

OFFICE
12' x 11'

CL

Up

MASTER
BEDROOM
15' x 15'

ENTRY   LAV

UTILITY

COVERED PORCH
(Included)

GARAGE
32' x 23'
(Optional)

Second floor

Open to Below

CL   CL

CL

CL

BEDROOM
15' x 12'

FAMILY ROOM
14' x 24'

Dn

BEDROOM
12' x 15'

B

CL   CL

Rear elevation

Dailey Design

The timeless appearance of the Dailey Design is accented with its large, covered entry porch and classic square columns. A second floor balcony as part of the family room provides views of the kitchen, dining, and great rooms. Optional built-in shelving in the great room, becomes a convenient place to showcase treasured books. An office on the main floor rounds out this home's classic approach.

BEDROOMS three + office

BATHROOMS 2 full + 1 half

MASTER BEDROOM first floor

TOTAL AREA 2,931 sq. ft.

FIRST FLOOR 1,894 sq. ft.

OTHER FLOOR 1,037 sq. ft.

SIZE 74' x 76'

0 feet   10 feet   20 feet

³⁄₆₄ inch represents 1 foot

⚠ Lindal

© Lindal Cedar Homes

Desert Rose

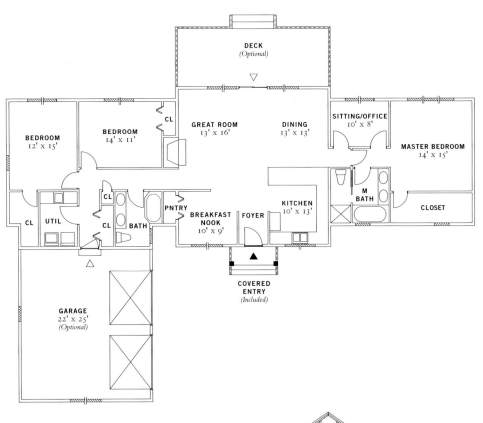

All-on-one floor design is distinctive of the Desert Rose. The separate breakfast nook creates a cozy, private haven to sip a warm beverage. Convenient access to a double-entry sitting room off the master suite is a unique feature. The large walk-in closet off the main bedroom can double as a dressing room.

BEDROOMS three + office

BATHROOMS 2 full

MASTER BEDROOM first floor

TOTAL AREA 1,953 sq. ft.

FIRST FLOOR 1,953 sq. ft.

SIZE 80' x 28'

0 feet · · · · 10 feet · · · · 20 feet

⅟₁₆ inch represents 1 foot

Rear elevation

△ **Lindal**

© *Lindal Cedar Homes*

First floor

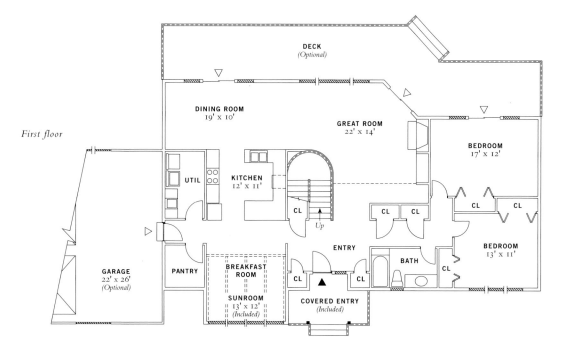

DECK
(Optional)

DINING ROOM
19' x 10'

GREAT ROOM
22' x 14'

BEDROOM
17' x 12'

UTIL

KITCHEN
12' x 11'

CL

CL   CL

CL   CL

Up

GARAGE
22' x 26'
(Optional)

PANTRY

BREAKFAST
ROOM

SUNROOM
13' x 12'
(Included)

CL

ENTRY

CL

BATH

CL

BEDROOM
13' x 11'

COVERED ENTRY
(Included)

Second floor

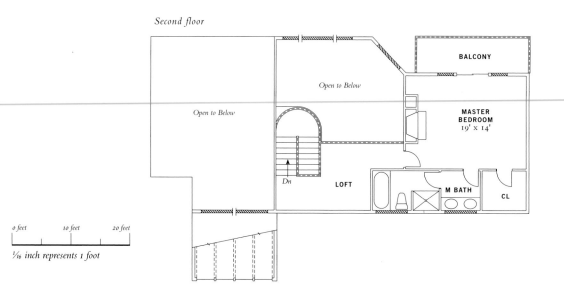

BALCONY

Open to Below

Open to Below

MASTER
BEDROOM
19' x 14'

Dn

LOFT

M BATH

CL

0 feet   10 feet   20 feet

⅟₁₆ inch represents 1 foot

DESIGNER

Sunburst

Sunburst's two-storied sunroom creates a warm, comfortable place during
the day and an enchanting spot for
evening hours. This home is literally
bursting with features. A loft located
on the upper floor, a master suite with
a balcony, a breakfast nook on the
main floor, and a walk-in pantry off
the kitchen round out the design of
this home. See photo ❶ 107.

BEDROOMS three

BATHROOMS 2 full

MASTER BEDROOM second floor

TOTAL AREA 2,475 sq. ft.

FIRST FLOOR 1,862 sq. ft.

OTHER FLOOR 613 sq. ft.

SIZE 82' x 37'

Rear elevation

⚠ Lindal

© *Lindal Cedar Homes*

First floor

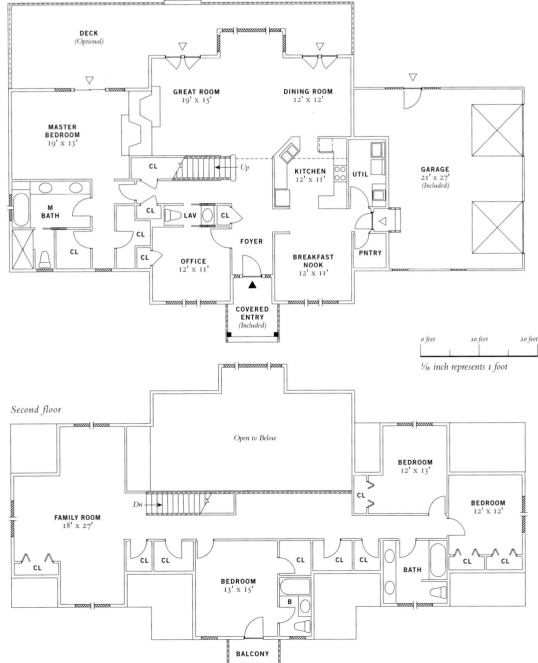

DECK
(Optional)

GREAT ROOM
19' x 15'

DINING ROOM
12' x 12'

MASTER
BEDROOM
19' x 13'

M
BATH

CL

Up

KITCHEN
12' x 11'

UTIL

GARAGE
21' x 27'
(Included)

CL

CL

LAV

CL

CL

CL

OFFICE
12' x 11'

FOYER

BREAKFAST
NOOK
12' x 11'

PNTRY

COVERED
ENTRY
(Included)

0 feet   10 feet   20 feet

1/16 inch represents 1 foot

Second floor

Open to Below

BEDROOM
12' x 13'

CL

BEDROOM
12' x 12'

FAMILY ROOM
18' x 27'

Dn

CL

CL

CL

CL

CL

BATH

CL

CL

BEDROOM
13' x 15'

B

BALCONY

Ellington

The Ellington is a smart looking home with a dramatic flair. A second story balcony provides dimension to this home's covered entry. The office is conveniently located next to the main entry. A breakfast nook and walk-in pantry make a cook's life a lot easier. See photos **L** 21, **L** 116, **L** 118, **P** 4, **P** 38, **P** 107.

BEDROOMS four + office
BATHROOMS 3 full + 1 half
MASTER BEDROOM first floor
TOTAL AREA 3,529 sq. ft.
FIRST FLOOR 1,955 sq. ft.
OTHER FLOOR 1,574 sq. ft.
SIZE 81' x 42'

Entry elevation

▲ Lindal

© Lindal Cedar Homes

Entry elevation

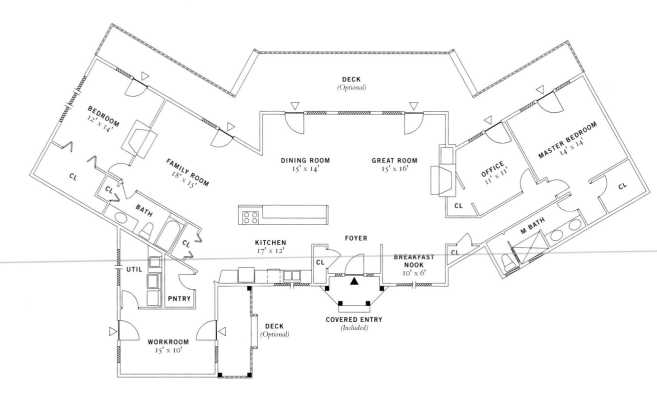

BEDROOM
12' x 14'

CL

FAMILY ROOM
18' x 15'

CL

CL

BATH

CL

DECK
(Optional)

DINING ROOM
15' x 14'

GREAT ROOM
15' x 16'

OFFICE
11' x 11'

CL

MASTER BEDROOM
14' x 14'

CL

UTIL

KITCHEN
17' x 12'

FOYER

CL

M BATH

CL

PNTRY

BREAKFAST
NOOK
10' x 6'

WORKROOM
15' x 10'

DECK
(Optional)

COVERED ENTRY
(Included)

Enlightened Log Home

With an exterior as great as the natural outdoors, the Enlightened Log Home brings a familiar rustic charm to its design. Its ground floor splendor offers large dining, family, and great rooms and a secluded office. The kitchen has its own walk-in pantry. The addition of optional solid cedar throughout the home creates an all-American interior beauty. Reference representative photograph ● 18.

BEDROOMS two + office

BATHROOMS 1 full + 1 three quarter

MASTER BEDROOM first floor

TOTAL AREA 2,462 sq. ft.

FIRST FLOOR 2,462 sq. ft.

SIZE 99' x 54'

0 feet   10 feet   20 feet

⅟₁₆ inch represents 1 foot

Muskoka

Muskoka's half-round covered porch off the dining room lends itself to unique entertaining possibilities. For instance, consider having the main meal inside, then moving to the great outdoors to enjoy dessert. This home's second floor passageway is a great place to take in an unobstructed view by looking out the great room's wall of windows.

BEDROOMS three

BATHROOMS 2 full + 1 half

MASTER BEDROOM first floor

TOTAL AREA 2,342 sq. ft.

FIRST FLOOR 1,472 sq. ft.

OTHER FLOOR 870 sq. ft.

SIZE 52' x 32'

0 feet   10 feet   20 feet

⅟₁₆ inch represents 1 foot

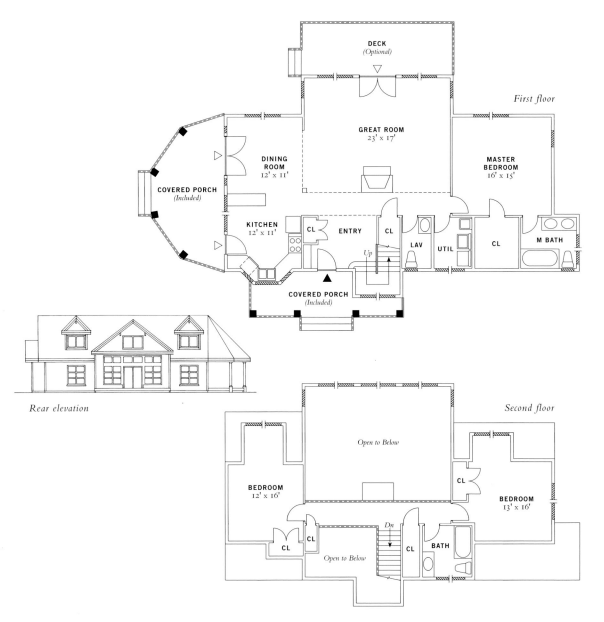

DECK
(Optional)

First floor

GREAT ROOM
23' x 17'

DINING
ROOM
12' x 11'

MASTER
BEDROOM
16' x 15'

COVERED PORCH
(Included)

KITCHEN
12' x 11'

CL   ENTRY   CL

LAV   UTIL   CL   M BATH

Up

COVERED PORCH
(Included)

Rear elevation

Second floor

Open to Below

BEDROOM
12' x 16'

CL

BEDROOM
13' x 16'

CL   CL

Dn   CL   BATH

Open to Below

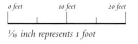

© Lindal Cedar Homes

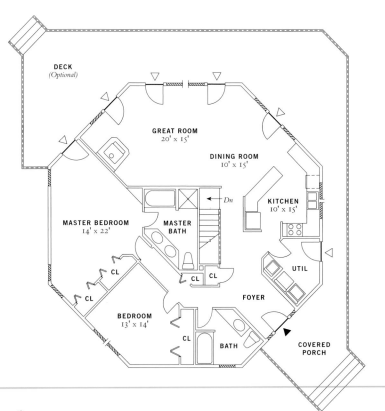

DECK
(Optional)

GREAT ROOM
20' x 15'

DINING ROOM
10' x 15'

Dn

KITCHEN
10' x 15'

MASTER BEDROOM
14' x 22'

MASTER
BATH

CL

CL

CL

CL

UTIL

BEDROOM
13' x 14'

CL

FOYER

CL

BATH

COVERED
PORCH

Octagon Oasis

This home's eight-sided design creates truly unique living spaces. Every inch of the Octagon Oasis is dedicated to providing the most efficient floorplan possible. Its master bathroom houses modern amenities such as a double sink and space for a separate shower and tub. The main living areas are open to each other and lend a feeling of space without boundaries.

BEDROOMS two

BATHROOMS 2 full

MASTER BEDROOM first floor

TOTAL AREA 1,564 sq. ft.

FIRST FLOOR 1,564 sq. ft.

SIZE 51' x 51'

0 feet	10 feet	20 feet

⅟₁₆ inch represents 1 foot

Rear/Side elevation

△ Lindal

© Lindal Cedar Homes

First floor

DECK
(Optional)

BEDROOM
15' x 12'

CL CL

BATH

DECK
(Optional)

BATH

MASTER BEDROOM
16' x 15'

GARAGE
24' x 32'
(Optional)

UTIL

KITCHEN
13' x 14'

P

DINING ROOM
13' x 19'

CL

CL

CL

GREAT ROOM
25' x 25'

CL

Up

CL LAV

FOYER

Up

BREAKFAST
NOOK
12' x 15'

CL

COVERED
ENTRY
(Included)

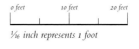

Rear elevation

Second floor

SKYWALL
(Included)

OFFICE
15' x 15'

BATH

Dn

CL

BEDROOM
18' x 19'

Open to Below

CL

Open to Below

Pine Hill Farm

The Pine Hill Farm is perfect for view lots with its expansive pavilion great room providing panoramic vistas. An extra bedroom upstairs with its own skywall makes an excellent place for visiting guests to relax. The main floor breakfast nook with its wall of windows creates an area to ponder the day ahead.

BEDROOMS three + office

BATHROOMS 3 full + 1 half

MASTER BEDROOM first floor

TOTAL AREA 2,979 sq. ft.

FIRST FLOOR 2,123 sq. ft.

OTHER FLOOR 856 sq. ft.

SIZE 73' x 57'

0 feet   10 feet   20 feet

⅟₁₆ inch represents 1 foot

Lindal

© *Lindal Cedar Homes*

111

Entry elevation

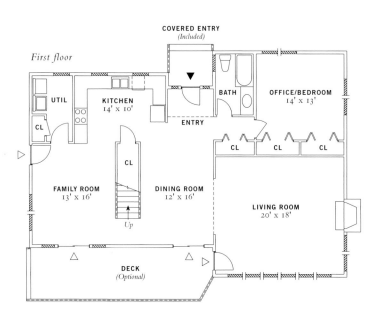

First floor

COVERED ENTRY
(Included)

UTIL

KITCHEN
14' x 10'

CL

CL

BATH

OFFICE/BEDROOM
14' x 13'

ENTRY

CL   CL   CL

FAMILY ROOM
13' x 16'

DINING ROOM
12' x 16'

LIVING ROOM
20' x 18'

Up

DECK
(Optional)

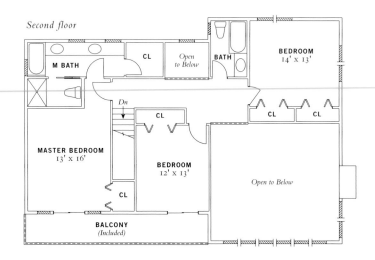

Second floor

M BATH

CL

Open to Below

BATH

BEDROOM
14' x 13'

Dn

CL

CL   CL

MASTER BEDROOM
13' x 16'

BEDROOM
12' x 13'

Open to Below

CL

BALCONY
(Included)

Springfield

The Springfield's soaring windows provide an airy, infinite feeling of space in the main floor living room. Add an optional deck for relaxing and watching an evening sunset. The relationship between family, dining and kitchen areas is continuous yet distinctive because of the central location of the stairs. The master suite's second story balcony is perfect for enjoying soft spring breezes.

BEDROOMS three + office

BATHROOMS 3 full

MASTER BEDROOM second floor

TOTAL AREA 2,539 sq. ft.

FIRST FLOOR 1,495 sq. ft.

OTHER FLOOR 1,044 sq. ft.

SIZE 48' x 35'

0 feet   10 feet   20 feet

¹⁄₁₆ inch represents 1 foot

⛰ Lindal

© *Lindal Cedar Homes*

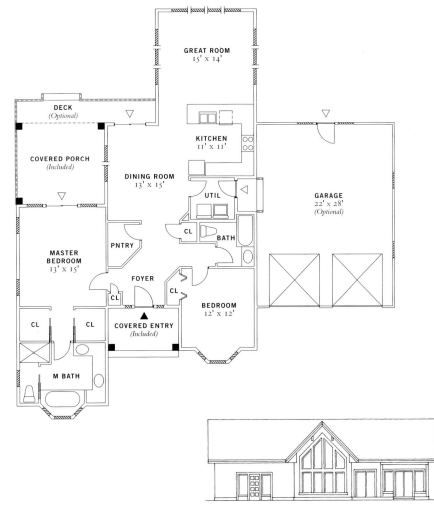

GREAT ROOM
15' x 14'

DECK
(Optional)

COVERED PORCH
(Included)

KITCHEN
11' x 11'

DINING ROOM
13' x 15'

UTIL

GARAGE
22' x 28'
(Optional)

PNTRY

CL

BATH

MASTER
BEDROOM
13' x 15'

FOYER

CL

CL

CL

CL

COVERED ENTRY
(Included)

BEDROOM
12' x 12'

M BATH

Trellis House

Perfectly suited for placement on narrow lots, the Trellis House combines old-fashioned values with a modern look. A covered porch entry with a trellis roof section provides a unique and welcoming appeal. A set of bay windows offers a comforting feeling from the past. A covered porch off the master bedroom is a special feature sure to become a favorite spot to relax and rejuvenate.

BEDROOMS two

BATHROOMS 2 full

MASTER BEDROOM first floor

TOTAL AREA 1,478 sq. ft.

FIRST FLOOR 1,478 sq. ft.

SIZE 60' x 63'

0 feet   10 feet   20 feet

⅟₁₆ inch represents 1 foot

113

Rear elevation

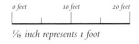

△ Lindal

© Lindal Cedar Homes

First floor

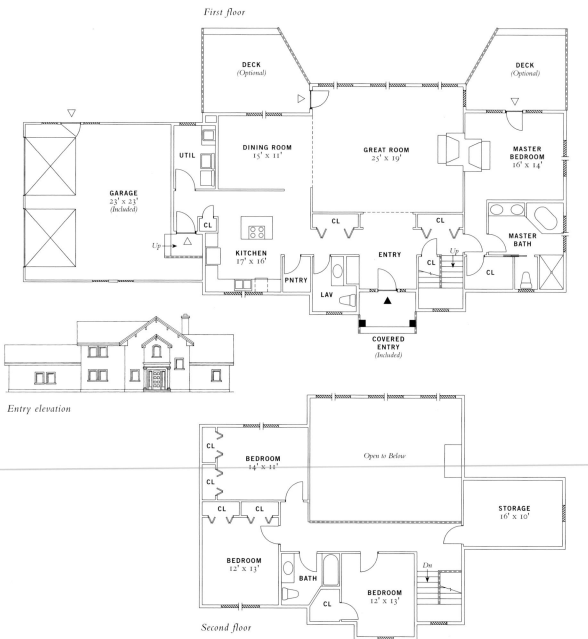

DECK
(Optional)

DECK
(Optional)

UTIL

DINING ROOM
15' x 11'

GREAT ROOM
25' x 19'

MASTER
BEDROOM
16' x 14'

GARAGE
23' x 23'
(Included)

CL

CL

CL

MASTER
BATH

Up

KITCHEN
17' x 16'

PNTRY

LAV

ENTRY

CL

Up

CL

COVERED
ENTRY
(Included)

Entry elevation

Winslow Place

Winslow Place's elegant architectural style is evident from the first exterior view. The great room's wall of windows and the addition of two optional decks off the master suite and dining room create a wraparound view. Three upper floor bedrooms and a large storage area nicely finish this polished design.

BEDROOMS four
BATHROOMS 2 full + 1 half
MASTER BEDROOM first floor
TOTAL AREA 2,873 sq. ft.
FIRST FLOOR 1,862 sq. ft.
OTHER FLOOR 1,011 sq. ft.
SIZE 86' x 36'

CL

BEDROOM
14' x 11'

Open to Below

CL

STORAGE
16' x 10'

CL

CL

BEDROOM
12' x 13'

BATH

CL

BEDROOM
12' x 13'

Dn

Second floor

0 feet   10 feet   20 feet

¹⁄₁₆ inch represents 1 foot

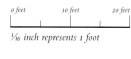

Woodbridge

Architectural balance is evident in Woodbridge's charming design. An eight-foot deep covered porch at its entry is a quaint place for sipping lemonade on a hot day. The spacious back covered porches have access to both the centrally located guest room and the impressive master bedroom. The office space and family room in the loft is an added bonus.

BEDROOMS two

BATHROOMS 2

MASTER BEDROOM first floor

TOTAL AREA 2,398 sq. ft.

FIRST FLOOR 1,751 sq. ft.

OTHER FLOOR 647 sq. ft.

SIZE 54' X 55'

0 feet   10 feet   20 feet

1/16 inch represents 1 foot

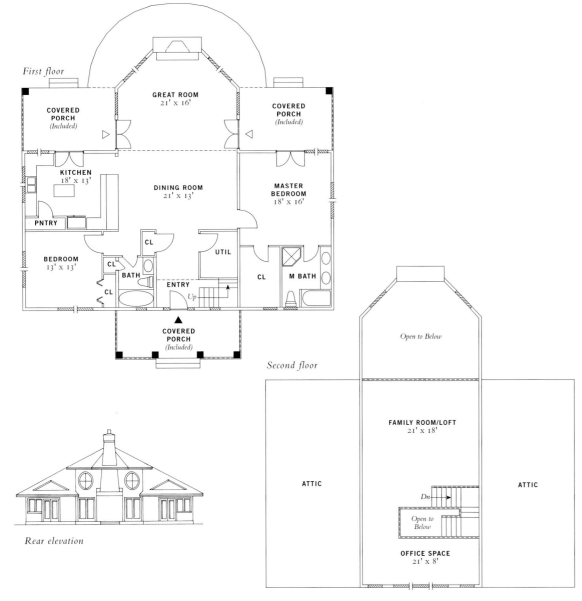

First floor

COVERED PORCH *(Included)*

GREAT ROOM 21' x 16'

COVERED PORCH *(Included)*

KITCHEN 18' x 13'

DINING ROOM 21' x 13'

MASTER BEDROOM 18' x 16'

PNTRY

CL

BEDROOM 13' x 13'

CL

CL

BATH

CL

UTIL

ENTRY

Up

CL

M BATH

COVERED PORCH *(Included)*

Rear elevation

Second floor

Open to Below

FAMILY ROOM/LOFT 21' x 18'

ATTIC

ATTIC

Dn

Open to Below

OFFICE SPACE 21' x 8'

Lindal

© *Lindal Cedar Homes*

Traditional

There aren't many opportunities in life to enjoy the best of the past and present. A Traditional Lindal is one of them. From the charms of Craftsman and Farmhouse designs to Colonial Revival, these are homes with a heritage. Inspired by the rich history of the most beloved architectural styles in North America, Traditional Lindal homes combine the style, quality materials and craftsmanship of yesterday with all the comforts and conveniences of today. Decorative posts, wraparound porches and gabled dormers create storybook street appeal; an easy flow of spacious, light-filled rooms makes them a joy to live in.

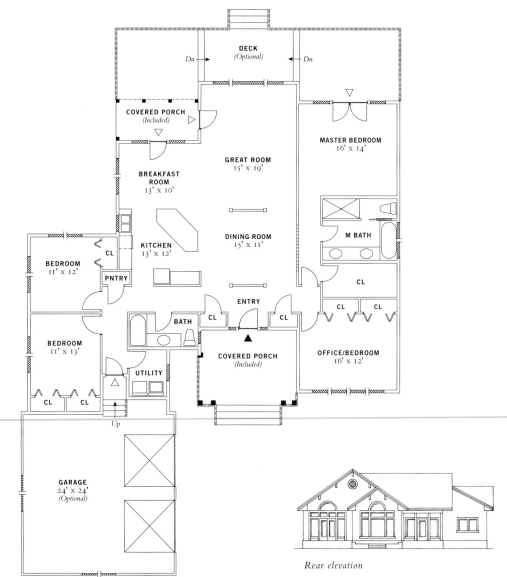

DECK
(Optional)

Dn   Dn

COVERED PORCH
(Included)

BREAKFAST
ROOM
13' x 10'

GREAT ROOM
15' x 19'

MASTER BEDROOM
16' x 14'

KITCHEN
13' x 12'

DINING ROOM
15' x 11'

M BATH

BEDROOM
11' x 12'

CL

PNTRY

CL

ENTRY

CL   CL

BATH

CL

CL

BEDROOM
11' x 13'

COVERED PORCH
(Included)

OFFICE/BEDROOM
16' x 12'

UTILITY

CL   CL

Up

GARAGE
24' x 24'
(Optional)

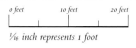

Rear elevation

Beaumont Place

Southern undertones are felt throughout Beaumont Place's elements. Impressive pillars lead to a covered porch entry. Arched windows provide a sense of grace and elegance. Housed all on the main level, this home's open, airy rooms lead and meld into one another creating a feeling of expanse. A covered porch opens into the breakfast room and great room offering shelter for eating or gathering.

BEDROOMS three + office

BATHROOMS 2 full

MASTER BEDROOM first floor

TOTAL AREA 1,998 sq. ft.

FIRST FLOOR 1,998 sq. ft.

SIZE 60' x 59'

0 feet   10 feet   20 feet

1/16 inch represents 1 foot

△ **Lindal**

© Lindal Cedar Homes

First floor

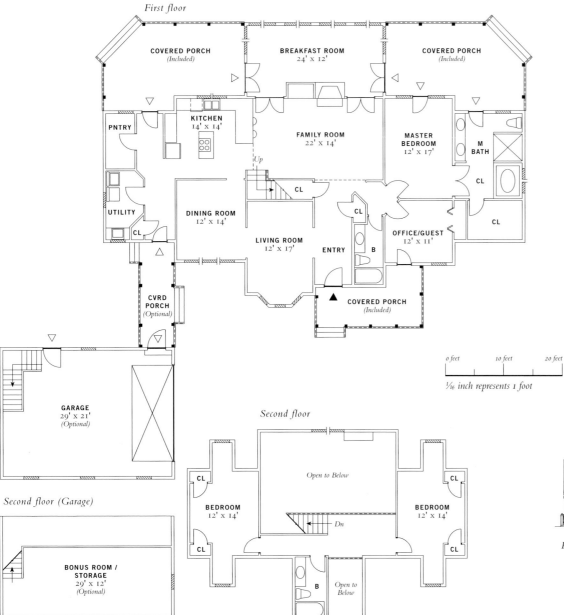

COVERED PORCH
(Included)

BREAKFAST ROOM
24' X 12'

COVERED PORCH
(Included)

PNTRY

KITCHEN
14' X 14'

FAMILY ROOM
22' X 14'

MASTER
BEDROOM
12' X 17'

M
BATH

CL

UTILITY

CL

DINING ROOM
12' X 14'

Up

CL

CL

CL

LIVING ROOM
12' X 17'

OFFICE/GUEST
12' X 11'

ENTRY

B

CVRD
PORCH
(Optional)

COVERED PORCH
(Included)

GARAGE
29' X 21'
(Optional)

Second floor (Garage)

BONUS ROOM /
STORAGE
29' X 12'
(Optional)

Second floor

CL

Open to Below

CL

BEDROOM
12' X 14'

Dn

BEDROOM
12' X 14'

CL

CL

B

Open to
Below

0 feet   10 feet   20 feet

1⁄16 inch represents 1 foot

Berkshire

High style is apparent in the Berkshire with details such as functional dormers in the two upstairs bedrooms and a bay window off the living room. Begin your day with morning meals in the sunny, open breakfast room. Two covered porches with access to the kitchen area on one side and the master bedroom on the other complete this classic treasure.

119

BEDROOMS three + office

BATHROOMS 3 full

MASTER BEDROOM first floor

TOTAL AREA 3,361 sq. ft.

FIRST FLOOR 2,313 sq. ft.

OTHER FLOOR 1,048 sq. ft.

SIZE 73' X 48'

Rear elevation

◮ Lindal

© Lindal Cedar Homes

First floor

COVERED PORCH

KITCHEN
15' x 14'

DECK
(Optional)

BREAKFAST NOOK
16' x 10'

GARAGE
24' x 24'
(Optional)

DINING ROOM
15' x 13'

PANTRY   UTILITY

CL

BATH

Laundry Chute

CL

GREAT ROOM
15' x 13'

Up

FOYER
15' x 7'

CL

OFFICE
11' x 11'

CL

CL

COVERED
ENTRY
(Included)

Second floor

COVERED PORCH

MASTER BEDROOM
15' x 14'

CL

M BATH

CL

BATH

Laundry Chute

CL

CL

Open to Below

Open to Below

Dn

BEDROOM
11' x 15'

Rear elevation

Brimfield

Traditional architecture is evident in Brimfield's dignified design. Modern details such as 18-foot high ceilings grace the dining and great rooms. Special features like a covered porch off the master suite, a breakfast nook separate from the dining area, and a home office complete this lovely home.

BEDROOMS two + office

BATHROOMS 3 full

MASTER BEDROOM second floor

TOTAL AREA 2,352 sq. ft.

FIRST FLOOR 1,460 sq. ft.

OTHER FLOOR 892 sq. ft.

SIZE 76' x 36'

0 feet   10 feet   20 feet

1/16 inch represents 1 foot

⏶ Lindal

© Lindal Cedar Homes

Bungalow Palani

Simpler times come to mind with the large covered porch of the quaint Bungalow Palani. A breakfast bar off the kitchen provides a convenient area for conversing with friends and family. Located in the back of the house, the master bedroom with its own private optional deck creates a relaxing refuge after a bustling day.

BEDROOMS two

BATHROOMS 2 full

MASTER BEDROOM first floor

TOTAL AREA 1,404 sq. ft.

FIRST FLOOR 1,404 sq. ft.

SIZE 51' X 51'

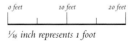

¹⁄₁₆ inch represents 1 foot

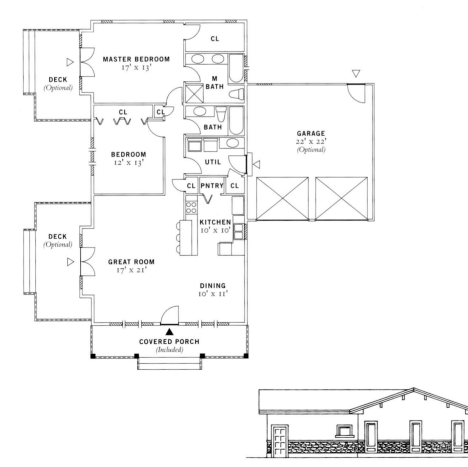

Rear elevation

© *Lindal Cedar Homes*

Camden Hill

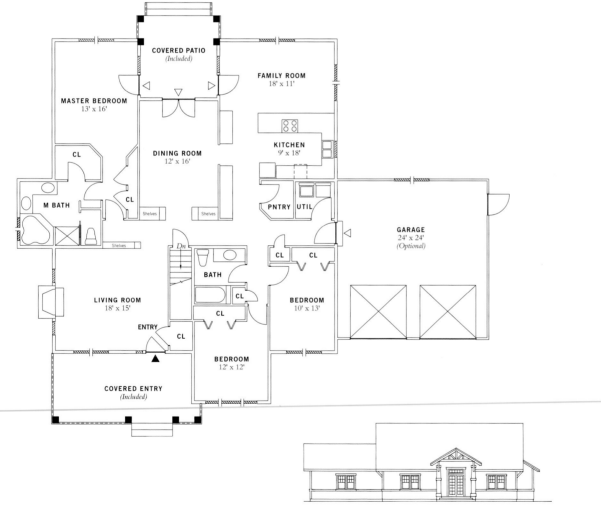

COVERED PATIO
(Included)

FAMILY ROOM
18' x 11'

MASTER BEDROOM
13' x 16'

CL

DINING ROOM
12' x 16'

KITCHEN
9' x 18'

CL

Shelves

Shelves

M BATH

CL

Shelves

PNTRY **UTIL**

GARAGE
24' x 24'
(Optional)

Dn

CL CL

BATH

CL

LIVING ROOM
18' x 15'

CL

BEDROOM
10' x 13'

ENTRY

CL

BEDROOM
12' x 12'

COVERED ENTRY
(Included)

The charming, old-fashioned exterior of the Camden Hill is captivatingly familiar. Its interior is filled with modern amenities and a well-zoned, one-level floorplan. A covered patio has entrances to both the master bedroom and family room. The large sheltered entry is a great place to add flower boxes and enhance this home's enchanting style.

BEDROOMS   three
BATHROOMS   2 full
MASTER BEDROOM   first floor
TOTAL AREA   2,197 sq. ft.
FIRST FLOOR   2,197 sq. ft.
SIZE   45' x 62'

0 feet   *10 feet*   *20 feet*

⅟₁₆ inch represents 1 foot

Rear elevation

⚠ **Lindal**

© *Lindal Cedar Homes*

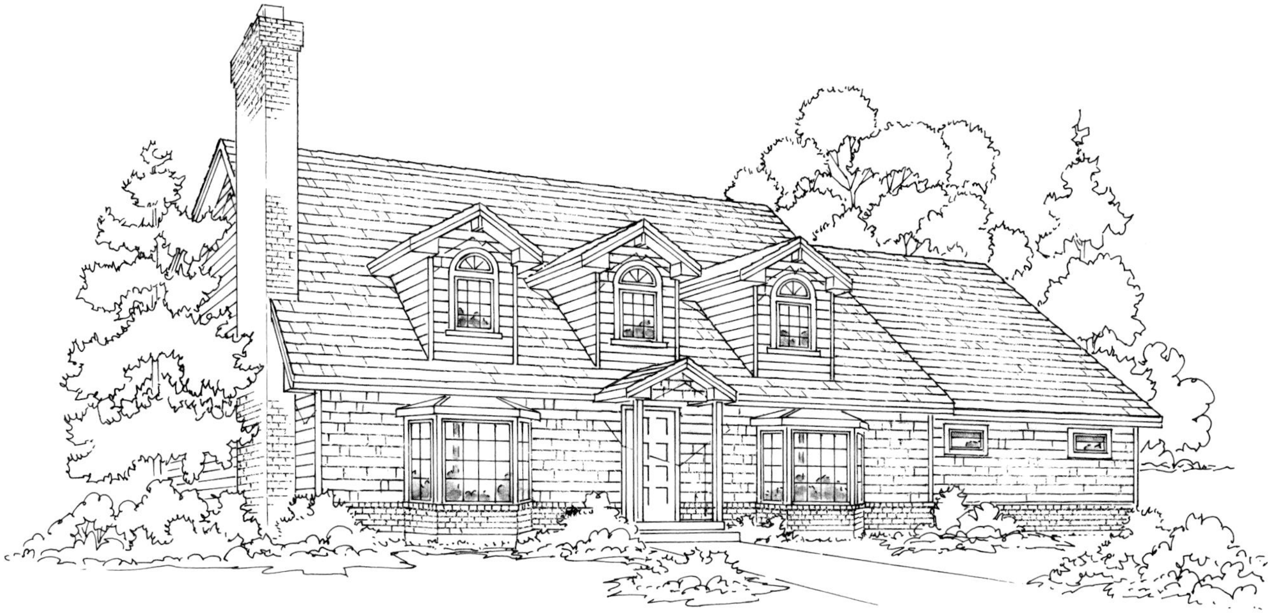

First floor

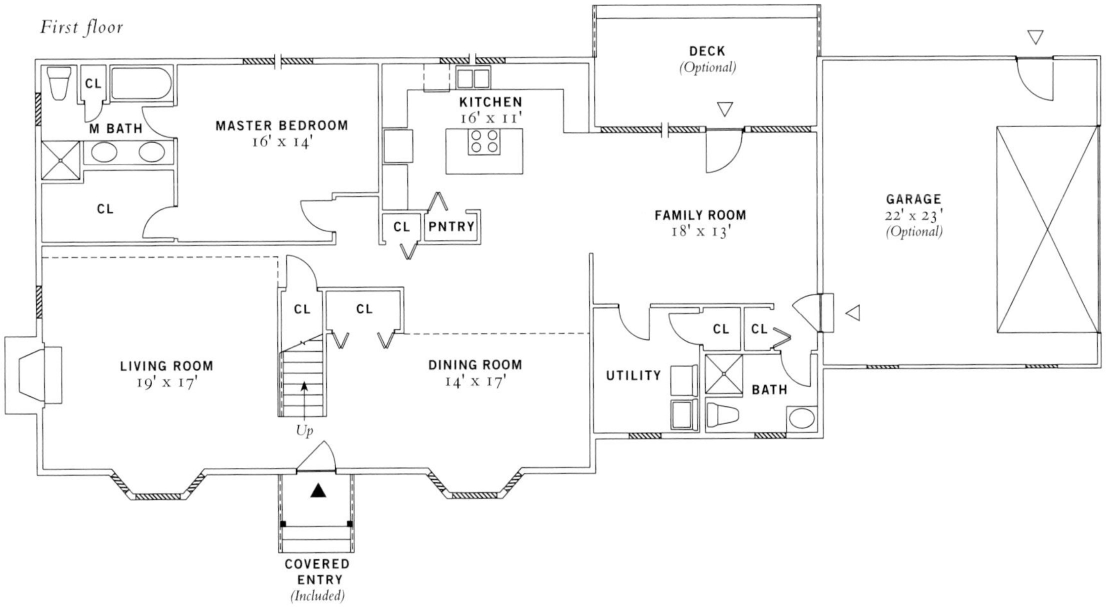
CL
M BATH
MASTER BEDROOM
16' x 14'
CL
KITCHEN
16' x 11'
DECK
(Optional)
CL
PNTRY
FAMILY ROOM
18' x 13'
GARAGE
22' x 23'
(Optional)
CL
CL
LIVING ROOM
19' x 17'
DINING ROOM
14' x 17'
UTILITY
CL
CL
BATH
Up
COVERED
ENTRY
(Included)

Second floor

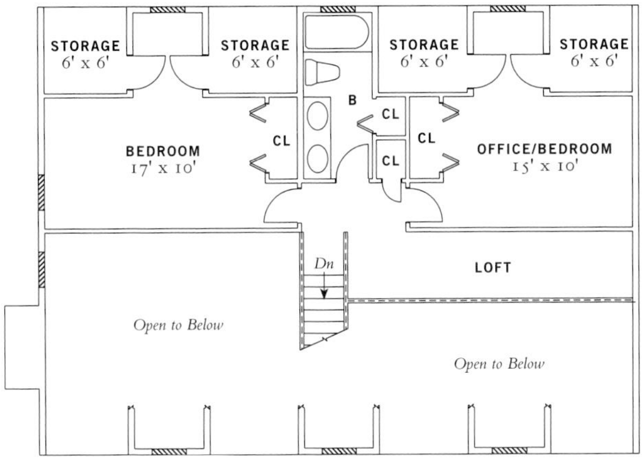
STORAGE
6' x 6'
STORAGE
6' x 6'
STORAGE
6' x 6'
STORAGE
6' x 6'
B
CL
CL
CL
CL
BEDROOM
17' x 10'
OFFICE/BEDROOM
15' x 10'
LOFT
Dn
Open to Below
Open to Below

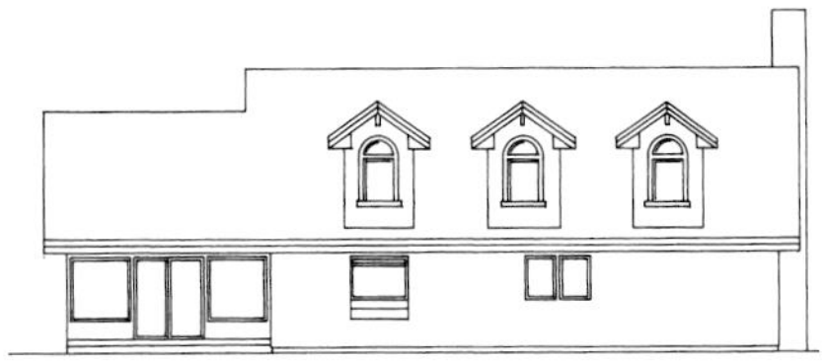

Rear elevation

Cape Breton

Inspired by the windswept beauty of the coast, the Cape Breton stands regally in any landscape. This elegant home contains two large bedrooms and an office, a loft on the upper floor and a family area separate from the living room. A railed balcony overlooking the main floor provides an infinite sense of openness. See photo Ⓛ 121.

BEDROOMS two + office
BATHROOMS 2 full + 1 three quarter
MASTER BEDROOM first floor
TOTAL AREA 2,533 sq. ft.
FIRST FLOOR 1,863 sq. ft.
OTHER FLOOR 670 sq. ft.
SIZE 84' x 34'

0 feet *10 feet* *20 feet*

1/16 inch represents 1 foot

Lindal

First floor

DECK
(Optional)

LIVING ROOM
20' x 16'

MASTER BEDROOM
16' x 13'

COVERED PORCH
(Included)

Up

CL

CL

KITCHEN
10' x 13'

UTIL

LAV

OFFICE
11' x 11'

M BATH

GARAGE
24' x 23'
(Optional)

PNTRY

ENTRY

CL   CL

CL

DINING ROOM
10' x 14'

COVERED PORCH
(Included)

Second floor

Open to Below

BEDROOM
10' x 13'

CL

CL

Dn

CL

Open to Below

B

BEDROOM
16' x 11'

CL

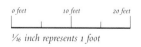

Rear elevation

Cottage Bluff

Cottage Bluff's warm charm permeates from the inside out. An extended covered porch housing the main entry welcomes visitors while providing shelter from the elements. A separate home office and utility room are nice additions. The master bedroom with its own covered porch becomes a tranquil spot to sit and watch the world go by.

BEDROOMS three + office
BATHROOMS 2 full + 1 half
MASTER BEDROOM first floor
TOTAL AREA 2,146 sq. ft.
FIRST FLOOR 1,549 sq. ft.
OTHER FLOOR 597 sq. ft.
SIZE 49' x 43'

0 feet   *10 feet*   *20 feet*

1/16 inch represents 1 foot

▲ **Lindal**

© *Lindal Cedar Homes*

Cumberland Cove

Cumberland Cove's sheltered entry and decorative trusses provide a craftsman flavor to this timeless design. A large master suite situated in the back of the house creates a space designated for privacy away from common areas. The remaining rooms are proportioned to create a balanced and open-feeling floorplan.

BEDROOMS two

BATHROOMS 2 full

MASTER BEDROOM first floor

TOTAL AREA 1,521 sq. ft.

FIRST FLOOR 1,521 sq. ft.

SIZE 45' x 55'

0 feet   10 feet   20 feet

1/16 inch represents 1 foot

Rear elevation

◢ **Lindal**

© *Lindal Cedar Homes*

Floor plan labels:

DECK (Optional)

MASTER BEDROOM 13' x 18'

CL

M BATH

GARAGE 24 x 24' (Optional)

CL

B

UTILITY

KITCHEN 15' x 10'

CL

BEDROOM 13' x 10'

CL

DINING ROOM 15' x 10'

GREAT ROOM 15' x 15'

COVERED ENTRY (Included)

First floor

DECK
(Optional)

UTIL

M
BATH

CL

KITCHEN
10' x 10'

LAV

CL

DINING ROOM
10' x 12'

CL

CL

MASTER
BEDROOM
14' x 15'

CL

CL

CL

LIVING ROOM
21' x 14'

Up

COVERED PORCH
(Included)

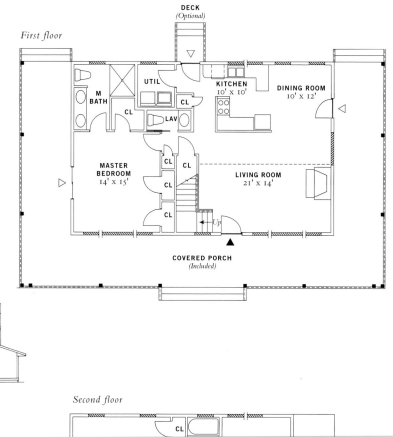

Rear elevation

Second floor

BEDROOM
16' x 10'

CL

CL

CL

CL

BATH

OFFICE/
FAMILY ROOM
17' x 15'

CL

CL

Dn

BEDROOM
14' x 12'

CL

CL

Open to Below

FARMHOUSE

Pioneer

One can almost smell freshly baked bread when viewing the Pioneer. A design with old-fashioned charm and modern appeal contained in one inviting package. The spacious master bedroom is conveniently located on the main floor. Extra space on the upper level is an excellent area to house a game room.

BEDROOMS three + office

BATHROOMS 1 full + 1 half + 1 3/4

MASTER BEDROOM first floor

TOTAL AREA 1,931 sq. ft.

FIRST FLOOR 1,120 sq. ft.

OTHER FLOOR 811 sq. ft.

SIZE 58' x 35'

0 feet   10 feet   20 feet

1/16 inch represents 1 foot

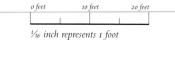

Lindal

© *Lindal Cedar Homes*

Rear elevation

First floor

DECK
(Optional)

DECK
(Optional)

LIVING ROOM
20' x 15'

DINING
ROOM

MASTER
BEDROOM
14' x 17'

CL

CL

SUNROOM
(Included)

BREAKFAST
NOOK
13' x 16'

CL

CL

M BATH

KITCHEN
17' x 17'

FOYER

OFFICE
10' x 10'

Up

CL

UTIL

CL

BATH

GARAGE
35' x 24'
(Optional)

BREEZEWAY
(Optional)

COVERED
ENTRY

Second floor

Open to Below

BEDROOM
14' x 11'

BEDROOM
14' x 11'

Dn

CL

CL

BATH

CL

CL

GAME ROOM
18' x 15'

Open to
Below

CL

CL

BEDROOM
14' x 15'

CL

Highlander

Highlander's handsome, sharp-looking exterior gives it an edge over other designs. An arched entryway leads to unobstructed views through towering living room windows. The breakfast nook with sunroom is a nice addition. An optional breezeway is a convenient way to stay dry when going from house to garage. A game room and an office round out this striking home.

BEDROOMS four + office

BATHROOMS 3 full

MASTER BEDROOM first floor

TOTAL AREA 3,299 sq. ft.

FIRST FLOOR 2,045 sq. ft.

OTHER FLOOR 1,254 sq. ft.

SIZE 56' x 46'

0 feet   10 feet   20 feet

3/64 inch represents 1 foot

Lindal

© *Lindal Cedar Homes*

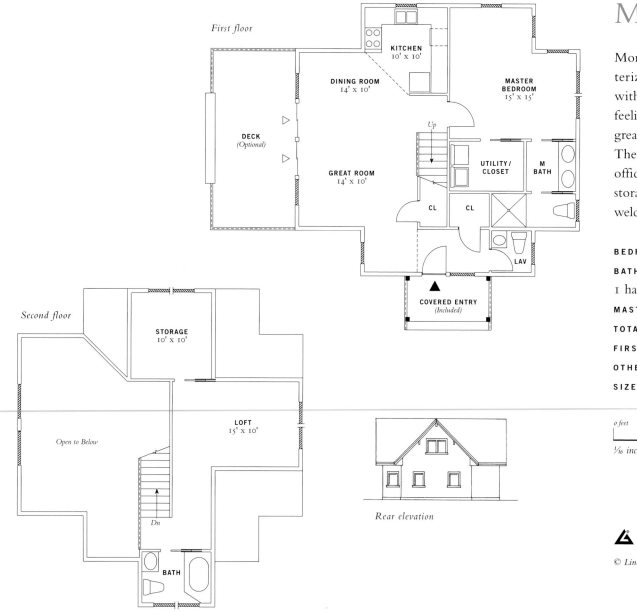

First floor

KITCHEN
10' X 10'

DINING ROOM
14' X 10'

MASTER
BEDROOM
15' X 15'

Up

DECK
(Optional)

GREAT ROOM
14' X 10'

UTILITY /
CLOSET

M
BATH

CL

CL

LAV

COVERED ENTRY
(Included)

Second floor

STORAGE
10' X 10'

LOFT
15' X 10'

Open to Below

Dn

BATH

Rear elevation

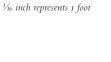

Morningside

Morningside's quaint look is characterized by a covered entry flanked with detailed posts. An expansive feeling pervades throughout the open great room, dining, and kitchen areas. The loft is a great space to add a home office, or cozy guest bedroom. Extra storage on the upper level is always a welcome addition.

BEDROOMS one

BATHROOMS 1 full +
1 half + 1 three-quarter

MASTER BEDROOM first floor

TOTAL AREA 1,456 sq. ft.

FIRST FLOOR 964 sq. ft.

OTHER FLOOR 492 sq. ft.

SIZE 35' X 32'

0 feet   10 feet   20 feet

¹⁄₁₆ inch represents 1 foot

Lindal

© *Lindal Cedar Homes*

Mountain House

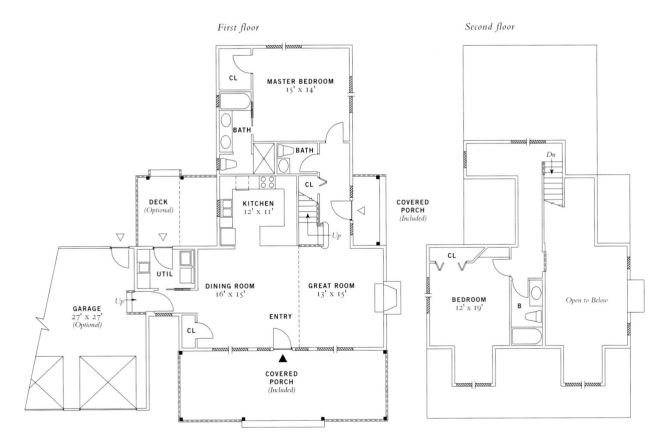

First floor

CL
MASTER BEDROOM
15' x 14'

BATH

BATH

CL

DECK
(Optional)

KITCHEN
12' x 11'

COVERED
PORCH
(Included)

UTIL

Up

GARAGE
27' x 27'
(Optional)

DINING ROOM
16' x 15'

GREAT ROOM
13' x 15'

Up

CL

ENTRY

COVERED
PORCH
(Included)

Second floor

Dn

CL

BEDROOM
12' x 19'

B

Open to Below

Rear elevation

Gabled dormers give The Mountain House a distinctively handsome look. Its large covered porch provides shelter during stormy weather and a place to listen to nature on calmer days. A rustic, relaxing demeanor is felt throughout the open great and dining rooms. The addition of a large old fashioned fireplace accentuates the charm of this design.

BEDROOMS two

BATHROOMS 2 full + 1 half

MASTER BEDROOM first floor

TOTAL AREA 1,710 sq. ft.

FIRST FLOOR 1,210 sq. ft.

OTHER FLOOR 500 sq. ft.

SIZE 43' x 57'

0 feet   10 feet   20 feet

⅟₁₆ *inch represents 1 foot*

▲ **Lindal**

© *Lindal Cedar Homes*

129

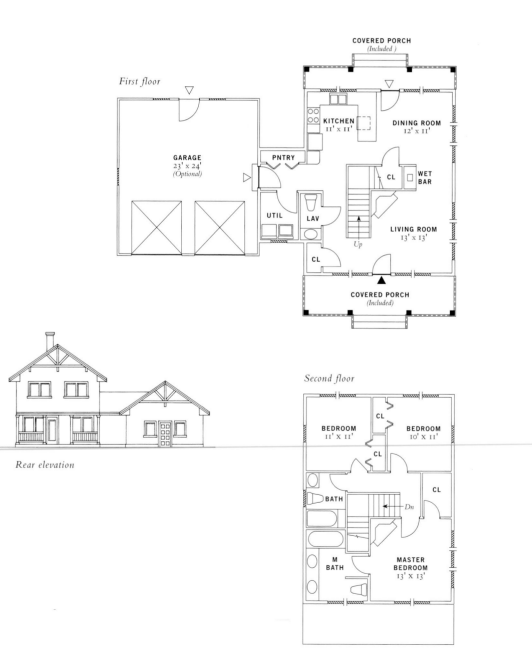

First floor

COVERED PORCH
(Included)

GARAGE
23' x 24'
(Optional)

KITCHEN
11' x 11'

DINING ROOM
12' x 11'

PNTRY

CL

WET BAR

UTIL

LAV

LIVING ROOM
13' x 13'

CL

Up

CL

COVERED PORCH
(Included)

Rear elevation

Second floor

BEDROOM
11' x 11'

CL

BEDROOM
10' x 11'

CL

BATH

CL

Dn

M BATH

MASTER BEDROOM
13' x 13'

Pecan Grove

Pecan Grove's graceful lines and crafts-man style are evident at first glance. This home takes every inch of its three bedroom, two and one-half bath floorplan and puts it to good use. The covered porch provides a great area for greeting your guests. Add an optional corner fireplace in the master suite to create a room where tensions melt away and relaxation takes priority.

BEDROOMS three
BATHROOMS 2 full + 1 half
MASTER BEDROOM second floor
TOTAL AREA 1,506 sq. ft.
FIRST FLOOR 785 sq. ft.
OTHER FLOOR 721 sq. ft.
SIZE 31' x 32'

0 feet   *10 feet*   *20 feet*

1/16 *inch represents 1 foot*

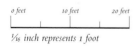 Lindal

© *Lindal Cedar Homes*

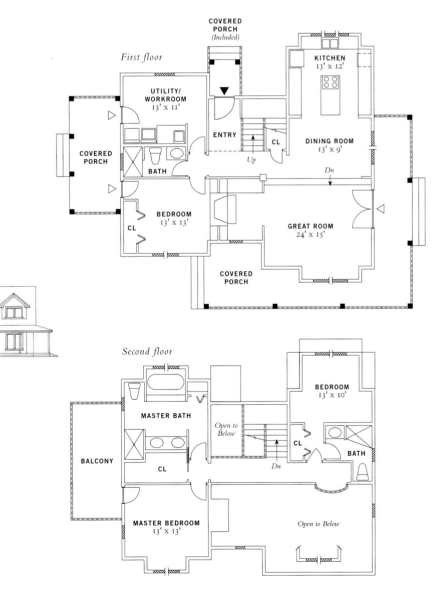

First floor

COVERED PORCH *(Included)*

UTILITY/ WORKROOM
13' x 11'

ENTRY

KITCHEN
13' x 12'

COVERED PORCH

BATH

Up

CL

DINING ROOM
13' x 9'

Dn

BEDROOM
13' x 13'

CL

GREAT ROOM
24' x 15'

COVERED PORCH

Second floor

MASTER BATH

Open to Below

BEDROOM
13' x 10'

BALCONY

CL

CL

BATH

Dn

MASTER BEDROOM
13' x 13'

Open to Below

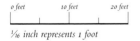

Rear elevation

Rosemont

Rosemont's enchanting traditional details draw you in at first glance. A covered porch wraps around the great room's exterior. Another has convenient access to the utility/work-room area. The upper floor master suite comes complete with its own balcony. High ceilings in the entryway and great room create a feeling of spaciousness in this compact design.

BEDROOMS three

BATHROOMS 1 full + 2 three quarter

MASTER BEDROOM second floor

TOTAL AREA 1,818 sq. ft.

FIRST FLOOR 1,194 sq. ft.

OTHER FLOOR 624 sq. ft.

SIZE 48' x 38'

0 feet   10 feet   20 feet

⅟₁₆ inch represents 1 foot

⊿ Lindal

© *Lindal Cedar Homes*

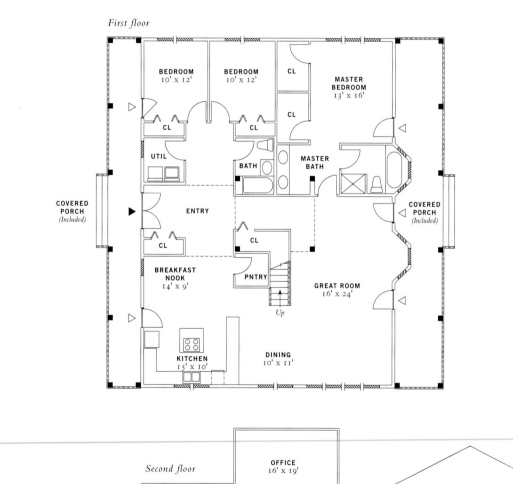

First floor

COVERED PORCH
(Included)

BEDROOM
10' x 12'

BEDROOM
10' x 12'

CL

MASTER BEDROOM
13' x 16'

CL

CL

CL

CL

UTIL

BATH

MASTER BATH

COVERED PORCH
(Included)

ENTRY

CL

BREAKFAST NOOK
14' x 9'

CL

PNTRY

GREAT ROOM
16' x 24'

Up

KITCHEN
15' x 10'

DINING
10' x 11'

Second floor

OFFICE
16' x 19'

Open to Below

Dn

CL

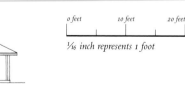

Rear elevation

Sandpiper Retreat

Clean, clear-cut lines with plenty of aesthetic appeal frame the Sandpiper Retreat. Pole construction allows for two full-length porches to embrace the front and back of the home, providing shelter from nature's elements. The office or added storage area is located on the upper floor. An abundance of windows in this home provides a light, airy feeling.

BEDROOMS three + office

BATHROOMS 2 full

MASTER BEDROOM first floor

TOTAL AREA 2,480 sq. ft.

FIRST FLOOR 2,158 sq. ft.

OTHER FLOOR 322 sq. ft.

SIZE 40' x 53'

0 feet   10 feet   20 feet

¹⁄₁₆ inch represents 1 foot

Lindal

© *Lindal Cedar Homes*

First floor

GARAGE
23' x 21'
(Optional)

DECK
(Optional)

MASTER
BEDROOM
13' x 15'

GREAT ROOM
21' x 18'

UTIL

KITCHEN
15' x 11'

M BATH

CL

CL CL

CL

CL

PNTRY

BREAKFAST
ROOM
12' x 12'

Up

ENTRY

CL

OFFICE
13' x 14'

LAV

CL

WET
BAR

DINING
ROOM
13' x 14'

COVERED ENTRY
(Included)

Second Floor

Open
to Below

Open
to Below

ATTIC

ATTIC

B

Dn

SHELVES

CL

Open to Below

ATTIC

BEDROOM
12' x 11'

Open to Below

Six Gables

Simple symmetry is at the heart of Six Gables' beauty and curbside appeal. A sheltered inset provides a main entry into the home. Inside, a breakfast room and walk-in pantry complement the kitchen area. A wet bar off the dining room is tucked into a convenient corner. An office located by the main entry completes this attractive home.

133

BEDROOMS two + office

BATHROOMS 2 full + 1 half

MASTER BEDROOM first floor

TOTAL AREA 2,556 sq. ft.

FIRST FLOOR 2,216 sq. ft.

OTHER FLOOR 340 sq. ft.

SIZE 52' x 47'

0 feet   10 feet   20 feet

3/64 inch represents 1 foot

Rear elevation

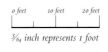

© Lindal Cedar Homes

Stone House Revival

Stone House Revival's handsome elements begin with its covered porch entry. A sunroom off the kitchen works well as a breakfast area. The sunken great room provides a formal element to this floorplan. A uniquely curved bay in the dining room is a nice touch. The spacious upper floor containing the master suite with an adjacent sitting room, complete this home's gracious design.

BEDROOMS four + sitting
BATHROOMS 2 full + 1 half
MASTER BEDROOM second floor
TOTAL AREA 4,128 sq. ft.
FIRST FLOOR 2,779 sq. ft.
OTHER FLOOR 1,349 sq. ft.
SIZE 79' x 55'

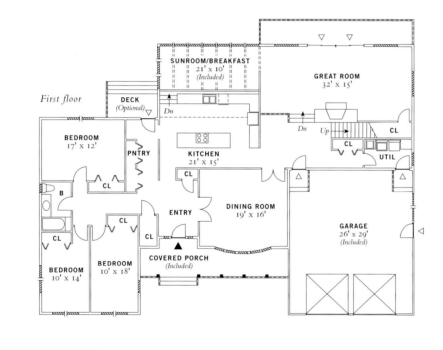

First floor

SUNROOM/BREAKFAST
21' x 10'
(Included)

GREAT ROOM
32' x 15'

DECK
(Optional)

Dn

Dn   Up   CL

CL

CL   UTIL

BEDROOM
17' x 12'

PNTRY

KITCHEN
21' x 15'

CL

B

CL

CL

ENTRY

DINING ROOM
19' x 16'

GARAGE
26' x 29'
(Included)

CL

CL   CL

BEDROOM
10' x 14'

BEDROOM
10' x 18'

COVERED PORCH
(Included)

Second floor

Rear elevation

Open to Below

BALCONY

LAV

Dn

MASTER
BATH

CL

CL

MASTER BEDROOM
27' x 21'

SITTING ROOM
26' x 15'

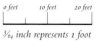

0 feet   10 feet   20 feet

3⁄64 inch represents 1 foot

▲ Lindal

© Lindal Cedar Homes

First floor

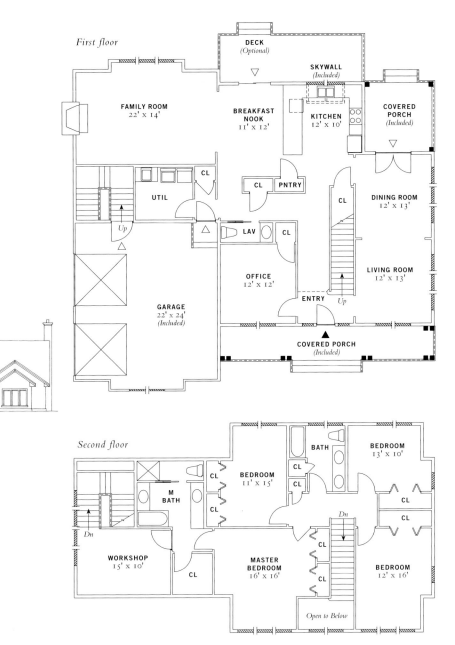

DECK
(Optional)

SKYWALL
(Included)

FAMILY ROOM
22' x 14'

BREAKFAST
NOOK
11' x 12'

KITCHEN
12' x 10'

COVERED
PORCH
(Included)

CL

UTIL

CL   PNTRY

CL

DINING ROOM
12' x 13'

CL

LAV   CL

OFFICE
12' x 12'

LIVING ROOM
12' x 13'

GARAGE
22' x 24'
(Included)

Up

ENTRY   Up

COVERED PORCH
(Included)

Rear elevation

Second floor

BATH

BEDROOM
13' x 10'

BEDROOM
11' x 15'

CL

CL

CL

CL

CL

CL

M
BATH

CL

CL

Dn

WORKSHOP
15' x 10'

CL

MASTER
BEDROOM
16' x 16'

CL

Dn

CL

BEDROOM
12' x 16'

Open to Below

Timberlake

The handsome details of the Timberlake begin with its double-column, covered porch housing the main entry. They continue on to windows that are placed to give a flood of light to the double height entryway. An office is conveniently located on the main floor. The kitchen's skywall is every cook's dream. A family room, two-car garage, and workshop with its own entry complete this special floorplan.

BEDROOMS four + office

BATHROOMS 2 full + 1 half

MASTER BEDROOM second floor

TOTAL AREA 3,118 sq. ft.

FIRST FLOOR 1,706 sq. ft.

OTHER FLOOR 1,412 sq. ft.

SIZE 57' x 51'

0 feet   10 feet   20 feet

1/16 *inch represents 1 foot*

▲ Lindal

© *Lindal Cedar Homes*

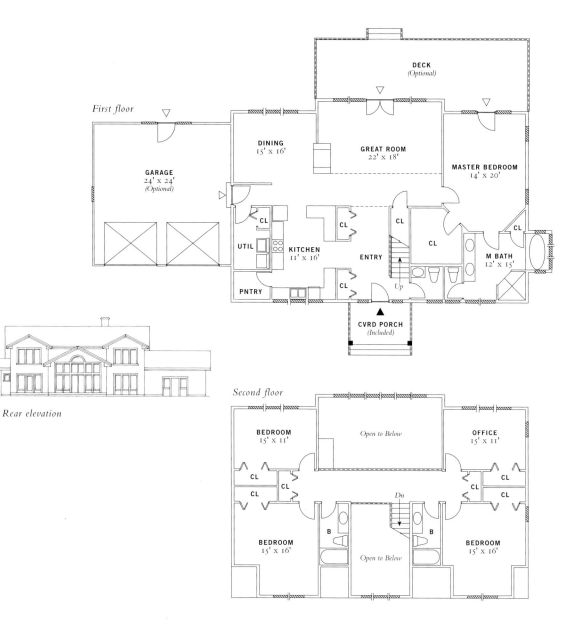

First floor

DECK
(Optional)

DINING
15' x 16'

GREAT ROOM
22' x 18'

MASTER BEDROOM
14' x 20'

GARAGE
24' x 24'
(Optional)

CL

CL

CL

CL

CL

CL

UTIL

KITCHEN
11' x 16'

ENTRY

CL

M BATH
12' x 15'

PNTRY

CL

Up

▲
CVRD PORCH
(Included)

Rear elevation

Second floor

BEDROOM
15' x 11'

Open to Below

OFFICE
15' x 11'

CL

CL

CL

CL

CL

CL

CL

CL

Dn

B

B

BEDROOM
15' x 16'

Open to Below

BEDROOM
15' x 16'

Trailwood Lodge

Smart-looking with stately features, the Trailwood Lodge offers inviting versatility. An optional expansive deck with easy access to the kitchen and adjacent to the great room provides a perfect place for outdoor parties. Indoor entertaining is enhanced with an addition of a double-sided fireplace. Nestled into the second floor is an office tucked in its own secluded corner.

BEDROOMS four + office

BATHROOMS 3 full + 1 half

MASTER BEDROOM first floor

TOTAL AREA 2,984 sq. ft.

FIRST FLOOR 1,721 sq. ft.

OTHER FLOOR 1,263 sq. ft.

SIZE 52' x 32'

0 feet   10 feet   20 feet

1/16 inch represents 1 foot

△ Lindal

© Lindal Cedar Homes

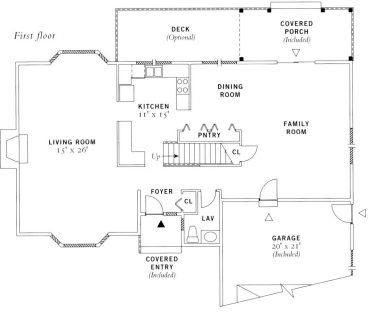

First floor

DECK
(Optional)

COVERED
PORCH
(Included)

DINING
ROOM

KITCHEN
11' X 15'

FAMILY
ROOM

LIVING ROOM
15' X 26'

PNTRY

CL

Up

FOYER

CL

LAV

COVERED
ENTRY
(Included)

GARAGE
20' X 21'
(Included)

Rear elevation

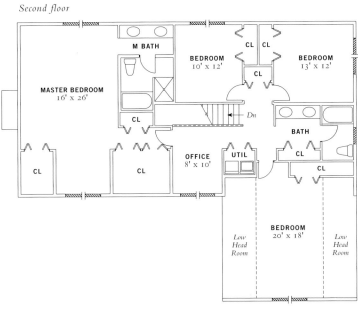

Second floor

M BATH

BEDROOM
10' X 12'

CL CL

CL

BEDROOM
13' X 12'

MASTER BEDROOM
16' X 26'

CL

Dn

BATH

CL

OFFICE
8' X 10'

UTIL

CL

CL

CL

CL

BEDROOM
20' X 18'

*Low
Head
Room*

*Low
Head
Room*

Cotswold

The traditional Tudor-styled Cotswold is built with room to roam. An expansive master suite on the upper level houses two walk-in closets and linen storage for the master bath. Three additional bedrooms and an office area complete the second story. The entry level contains a well-sized kitchen, dining, family, and living rooms.

137

BEDROOMS four + office

BATHROOMS 2 full + 1 half

MASTER BEDROOM second floor

TOTAL AREA 3,075 sq. ft.

FIRST FLOOR 1,340 sq. ft.

OTHER FLOOR 1,735 sq. ft.

SIZE 54' X 51'

0 feet   10 feet   20 feet

⅟₁₆ inch represents 1 foot

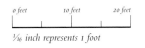

© *Lindal Cedar Homes*

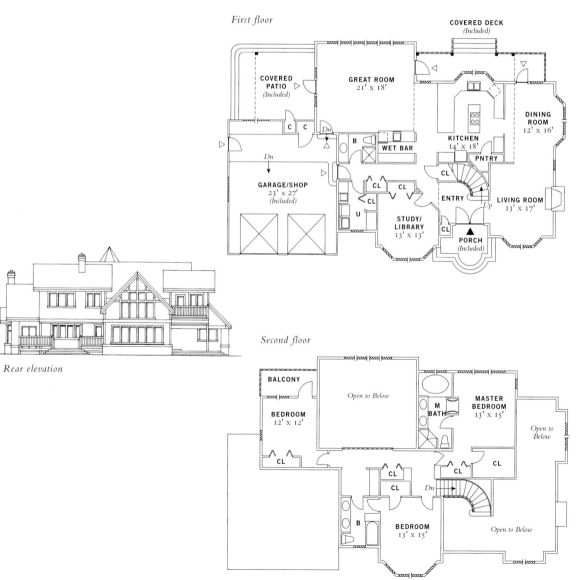

First floor

COVERED DECK
(Included)

COVERED PATIO
(Included)

GREAT ROOM
21' x 18'

DINING ROOM
12' x 16'

KITCHEN
14' x 18'

WET BAR

PNTRY

GARAGE/SHOP
23' x 27'
(Included)

LIVING ROOM
13' x 17'

ENTRY

STUDY/ LIBRARY
13' x 13'

PORCH
(Included)

Rear elevation

Second floor

BALCONY

Open to Below

MASTER BEDROOM
13' x 15'

M BATH

BEDROOM
12' x 12'

Open to Below

Open to Below

BEDROOM
13' x 15'

Open to Below

Jacob's Tudor

Jacobs Tudor is sure to catch many passing glances. On the main floor, a library has wonderful floor to ceiling windows in the lower portion of the turret. A great room with two-stories of windows and a covered patio and deck welcome indoor/outdoor entertaining. A balcony located off an upper floor bedroom is an attractive place to grab a breath of fresh air.

BEDROOMS three + library

BATHROOMS 2 full + 1 three quarter

MASTER BEDROOM second floor

TOTAL AREA 2,900 sq. ft.

FIRST FLOOR 1,748 sq. ft.

OTHER FLOOR 1,152 sq. ft.

SIZE 72' x 50'

0 feet   10 feet   20 feet

3/64 inch represents 1 foot

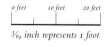

© Lindal Cedar Homes

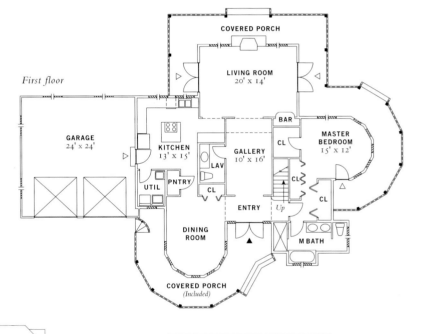

First floor

COVERED PORCH

LIVING ROOM
20' x 14'

GARAGE
24' x 24'

KITCHEN
13' x 15'

GALLERY
10' x 16'

BAR

CL

MASTER
BEDROOM
15' x 12'

LAV

UTIL

PNTRY

CL

CL

CL

CL

ENTRY

Up

M BATH

DINING
ROOM

COVERED PORCH
(Included)

Rear elevation

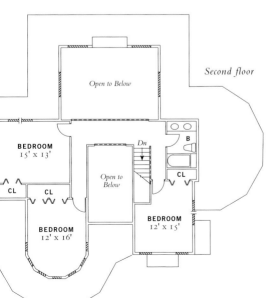

Second floor

Open to Below

BEDROOM
15' x 13'

Open to
Below

Dn

B

CL

CL

CL

CL

BEDROOM
12' x 16'

BEDROOM
12' x 15'

Victorian Rose

The Victorian Rose's old-world charm is evident in its historical style. Two uniquely shaped half-round rooms with corresponding covered porches add an original touch. A double-door entry leads to a gallery with an unobstructed view of the living room. A covered porch with two separate entries off the living room offers endless entertaining possibilities.

BEDROOMS four

BATHROOMS 2 full + 1 half

MASTER BEDROOM first floor

TOTAL AREA 2,497 sq. ft.

FIRST FLOOR 1,596 sq. ft.

OTHER FLOOR 901 sq. ft.

SIZE 50' x 45'

0 feet   10 feet   20 feet

³⁄₆₄ inch represents 1 foot

△ Lindal

© *Lindal Cedar Homes*

142

Ready for more ideas for your new home? Your *Lindal Living* and *Lindal Planning* books are just the beginning of the resources created for you by Lindal, the world's leading maker of custom cedar homes. Send for our latest CD-ROM — a rich planning guide with over 1,600 photographs, virtual home tours and interactive tools that help you bring your new home to life. And order your *Lindal SunRoom* planbook now — because, if you're like many Lindal homeowners, you'll find you want to make a sunroom central to your home planning. Of course, from dreaming through designing, the ultimate Lindal resource is your local independent Lindal dealer. For the name and location of the Lindal dealer nearest you, simply call us toll-free at 1.800.426.0536, or visit Lindal on the Web at: http://www.lindal.com.

Order Now! *(please check your selections)*

☐ LINDAL SUNROOM PLANBOOK
Plan a sunroom with this 27 page, full-color book and add beauty and value to your home. $3.00 (price includes U.S. Mail first class shipping rate.)

☐ CD-ROM
With virtual reality home tours, interactive home planning tools, 1600 photos and more. $12.95 (price includes U.S. Mail first class shipping rate.)

BUSINESS REPLY MAIL
FIRST-CLASS MAIL   PERMIT NO. 9943   SEATTLE, WA

POSTAGE WILL BE PAID BY ADDRESSEE

Lindal
CEDAR HOMES

P.O. BOX 24426
SEATTLE WA 98124-0426